RECAP

APPLY

REVIEW

SUCCEED

REVISION GUIDE

AQA

GCSE

Religious Studies A (9 – 1)

Christianity

Marianne Fleming
Peter Smith

OXFORD

UNIVERSITY PRESS

ACKNOWLEDGEMENTS

The publishers would like to thank the following for permissions to use their photographs:

Cover: Image Source/Getty Images

Artworks: QBS Learning and Jason Ramasami

Photos: p16: Renata Sedmakova/Shutterstock; **p17**: GrahamMoore999/iStockphoto; **p60**: mshch/iStock; **p61**: Kampol Taepanich/Shutterstock; **p83**: CARL DE SOUZA/AFP/Getty Images; **p96**: zendograph/Shutterstock; **p106**: Yuriy Boyko/Shutterstock; **p109**: Michael Ochs Archives/Getty Images; **p112**: Mamunur Rashid/Alamy Stock Photo; **p113**: Jim West/Alamy Stock Photo;

We are grateful to the authors and publishers for use of extracts from their titles and in particular for the following:

Scripture quotations [marked NIV] taken from the **Holy Bible, New International Version Anglicised** Copyright © 1979, 1984, 2011 Biblica. Used by permission of Hodder & Stoughton Ltd, an Hachette UK company. All rights reserved. 'NIV' is a registered trademark of Biblica UK trademark number 1448790.; **Anglican Pacifists:** *Anglican Pacifist Fellowship (APF)'s Pledge,* http://anglicanpeacemaker.org.uk/wp-content/uploads/2015/11/TAP-Oct-2015.pdf (Anglican Pacifist Fellowship, 2015). Reproduced with permission from Anglican Pacifist Fellowship.; **AQA:** *Paper 1A: Specimen question paper,* (AQA 2017). Reproduced with permission from AQA.; **AQA:** *Paper 1A: Additional specimen question paper,* (AQA 2017). Reproduced with permission from AQA.; **The Church of England:** Lines from the *Creeds,* the *Lord's Prayer,* the *marriage rite* and the *baptism rite.* (The Archbishops' Council, 2017). © The Archbishops' Council. Reproduced with permission from The Archbishops' Council. ; **The Church of England:** *The Lambeth Conference: Resolutions Archive from 1930,* (Anglican Communion Office, 2005). © The Archbishops' Council. Reproduced with permission from The Archbishops' Council. ; **The Church of England:** *Marriage, Family & Sexuality Issues,* https://www.churchofengland.org/our-views/marriage,-family-and-sexuality-issues/family.aspx (The Archbishops' Council, 2010). © The Archbishops' Council. Reproduced with permission from The Archbishops' Council. ; **S. Hucklesby:** 'Mutual cooperation, not mutual destruction' say Churches, The Methodist Church in Britain website, 23rd May 2015. http://www.methodist.org.uk/news-and-events/news-releases/mutual-cooperation-not-mutual-destruction-say-churches (The Methodist Church in Britain, 2015). © Trustees for Methodist Church Purposes. Reproduced with permission from The Methodist Church in Britain. ; **Pope Francis:** quote from speech October 2014. (The Vatican, 2014). © Libreria Editrice Vaticana. Reproduced with permission from The Vatican. ; **Pope Francis:** quote from Mass June 2015. (The Vatican, 2015). Reproduced with permission from The Vatican. © Libreria Editrice Vaticana.; **Pope Paul VI:** *Humanae Vitae,* (The Vatican, 1968). © Libreria Editrice Vaticana. Reproduced with permission from The Vatican.; **The Vatican:** *Catechism of the Catholic Church,* (The Vatican 1993). © Libreria Editrice Vaticana. Reproduced with permission from The Vatican. ; **Father L. Serrini:** *The Christian Declaration on Nature,* (Alliance of Religions and Conservation (ARC), 1986). Reproduced with permission from ARC.; **The United Nations:** The Universal Declaration of Human Rights, (UDHR) (United Nations, 1948). Reproduced with permission from United Nations.

We have made every effort to trace and contact all copyright holders before publication, but if notified of any errors or omissions, the publisher will be happy to rectify these at the earliest opportunity.

Contents

PART ONE: THE STUDY OF RELIGIONS.................... 12

How
exam-ready
are you?

😞 😐 ☺

Introduction

What will the exam be like?

For your GCSE Religious Studies exam, you will sit two papers.

- **Paper 1 will cover the study of religions.** You will need to answer questions on the beliefs and teachings, and practices, of **two** world religions. There will be separate question and answer booklets for each religion. Chapters 1 and 2 of this revision guide will help you to answer questions on Christianity for Paper 1. In addition, you will need to answer questions on a second religion, which might be Buddhism, Hinduism, Islam, Judaism or Sikhism.

- **Paper 2 will cover thematic studies.** There are six themes on the paper. You will need to **choose four themes**, and answer all the questions for each chosen theme. You will need to know about religious beliefs and viewpoints on themes and issues. Except in those questions where the main religious tradition of Great Britain is asked for, you can use beliefs from any religion in your answer. For example, you might want to focus on Christianity, including viewpoints from different traditions within Christianity, such as Catholic or Protestant views. Or you might want to include beliefs from other religions, such as Buddhist, Hindu, Muslim, Jewish or Sikh viewpoints. Chapters 3 to 8 of this revision guide cover the six themes, focusing on a Christian perspective.

If you are studying **St Mark's Gospel**, then the six themes will appear in Section A of Paper 2. You will need to choose **two themes**. You will then also need to answer the **two questions on St Mark's Gospel** from Section B.

> **TIP**
>
> Each paper is 1 hour and 45 minutes long, and you'll need to answer four full questions. Aim to spend 25 minutes on each question.

What kind of questions will be on the exam?

Each question on the exam will be split into five parts, worth 1, 2, 4, 5 and 12 marks.

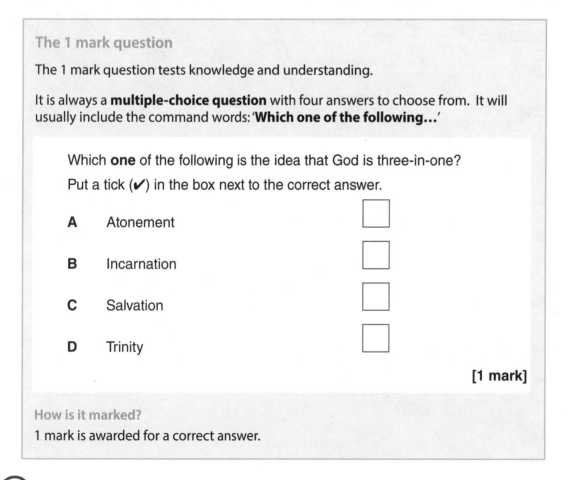

The 1 mark question

The 1 mark question tests knowledge and understanding.

It is always a **multiple-choice question** with four answers to choose from. It will usually include the command words: '**Which one of the following...**'

> Which **one** of the following is the idea that God is three-in-one?
>
> Put a tick (✔) in the box next to the correct answer.
>
> **A**   Atonement ☐
>
> **B**   Incarnation ☐
>
> **C**   Salvation ☐
>
> **D**   Trinity ☐
>
> **[1 mark]**

How is it marked?
1 mark is awarded for a correct answer.

The 2 mark question

The 2 mark question tests knowledge and understanding.

It always begins with the command words 'Give two...' or 'Name two...'

Give **two** ways in which religious believers help victims of war.

[2 marks]

How is it marked?
1 mark is awarded for 1 correct point.
2 marks are awarded for 2 correct points.

TIP

The examiner is expecting two simple points, not detailed explanations. You would get 2 marks if you answered "1) praying for victims; 2) providing food and shelter". You don't need to waste time by writing in full sentences and giving long explanations.

The 4 mark question

The 4 mark question tests knowledge and understanding.

It always begins with the command words 'Explain two...'

It might test your knowledge of how a religion influences individuals, communities and societies. Or it might ask for similarities or differences within or between religions.

TIP

Here, 'contrasting' means different. The question is asking you to explain two different ways in which Holy Communion is celebrated.

Explain **two** contrasting ways in which Holy Communion is celebrated in Christianity.

[4 marks]

How is it marked?
For the first way, influence or similar/contrasting belief:

- 1 mark is awarded for a simple explanation
- 2 marks are awarded for a detailed explanation.

For the second way, influence or similar/contrasting belief:

- 1 mark is awarded for a simple explanation
- 2 marks are awarded for a detailed explanation.

So for the full 4 marks, the examiner is looking for two ways/influences/ beliefs and for you to give detailed explanations of both. The examiner is expecting you to write in full sentences.

What is a detailed explanation?

An easy way to remember what you need to do for the four mark question is:

Make one point > **Develop it**

Make a second point > **Develop it**

TIP

One point you might make to answer this question is to say "Catholics celebrate Holy Communion by receiving offerings of bread and wine." This would get you 1 mark. For a second mark you could develop the point by giving further information: "During the service they believe the bread and wine become the body and blood of Jesus Christ."

There is more you could probably say, but as you'd get 2 marks for this, it would be better to turn your attention to thinking about a second contrasting way in which Holy Communion is celebrated, and then developing that second point.

But how do you develop a point? You might do this by:

- giving more information
- giving an example
- referring to a religious teaching or quotation.

The 'Great Britain' question

Sometimes there may be additional wording to the 4 mark question, asking you to **'Refer to the main religious tradition of Great Britain and one or more other religious traditions.'**

> Explain **two** similar religious beliefs about abortion.
>
> In your answer you should refer to the main religious tradition of Great Britain and one or more other religious traditions.
>
> **[4 marks]**

The main religious tradition of Great Britain is Christianity, so in your answer **you must refer to Christianity**. You can refer to **two different denominations within Christianity**, or you can compare **a Christian belief with that from another religion,** such as Buddhism, Hinduism, Islam, Judaism or Sikhism.

For theme C: the existence of God and revelation, the wording will say: 'In your answer you should refer to the main religious tradition of Great Britain **and non-religious beliefs.**' You must refer to Christianity and a non-religious belief.

This type of question will only be asked about certain topics. We point them out in this Revision Guide using this feature:

> You might be asked to compare beliefs on contraception between Christianity (the main religious tradition in Great Britain) and another religious tradition.

TIP

You can't, for example, refer to two different groups within Buddhism, or compare Buddhism and Islam. There must be a reference to Christianity or you won't get full marks for this question however detailed your answer is.

The 5 mark question

The 5 mark question tests knowledge and understanding.

Like the 4-mark question, it always begins with the command words **'Explain two…'** In addition it will also ask you to **'Refer to sacred writings or another source of religious/Christian belief and teaching in your answer.'**

> Explain **two** reasons why Christians pray.
>
> Refer to sacred writings or another source of Christian belief and teaching in your answer.
>
> **[5 marks]**

How is it marked?

For the first reason/teaching/belief:

- 1 mark is awarded for a simple explanation
- 2 marks are awarded for a detailed explanation.

For the second reason/teaching/belief:

- 1 mark is awarded for a simple explanation
- 2 marks are awarded for a detailed explanation.

Plus 1 mark for a relevant reference to sacred writings or another source of religious belief.

So for the full 5 marks, the examiner is looking for two reasons/teachings/beliefs and for you to give detailed explanations of both, just like the 4 mark question. **For the fifth mark, you need to make reference to a writing or teaching that is considered holy or authoritative by a religion.** The examiner is expecting you to write in full sentences. You might aim to write five sentences.

What counts as 'sacred writings or another source of religious belief and teaching'?

Sacred writings and religious beliefs or teachings might include:

- a quotation from a holy book (e.g. the Bible)
- a statement of religious belief such as the Apostles' Creed
- a prayer such as the Lord's prayer
- a statement made by a religious leader, for example the Pope
- a quotation from a religious text such as the Catechism of the Catholic Church.

> **TIP**
>
> If you can quote exact phrases this will impress the examiner, but if you can't then it's fine to paraphrase. It's also ok if you can't remember the exact verse that a quotation is from, but it would be helpful to name the holy book, for example, to specify that it is a teaching from the Bible.

The 12 mark question

The 12 mark question tests analytical and evaluative skills. It will always begin with a statement, and then ask you to **evaluate the statement**. There will be bullet points guiding you through what the examiner expects you to provide in your answer.

From Paper 1:

> 'The Bible tells Christians all they need to know about God's creation.'
>
> Evaluate this statement. In your answer you should:
>
> - refer to Christian teaching
> - give reasoned arguments to support this statement
> - give reasoned arguments to support a different point of view
> - reach a justified conclusion.
>
> **[12 marks]**
> **[+3 SPaG marks]**

> **TIP**
>
> The examiners are not just giving marks for what you know, but for your ability to weigh up different sides of an argument, making judgements on how convincing or weak you think they are. The examiner will also be looking for your ability to connect your argument logically.

From Paper 2:

'War is never right'

Evaluate this statement. In your answer you:

- should give reasoned arguments in support of this statement
- should give reasoned arguments to support a different point of view
- should refer to religious arguments
- may refer to non-religious arguments
- should reach a justified conclusion.

[12 marks]

[+3 SPaG marks]

TIP

For Paper 2, on thematic issues, you can use different views from one or more religions, and you can also use non-religious views.

How is it marked?

Level	What the examiner is looking for	Marks
4	A well-argued response with two different points of view, both developed to show a logical chain of reasoning that leads to judgements supported by relevant knowledge and understanding. *References to religion applied to the issue.*	10–12 marks
3	Two different points of view, both developed through a logical chain of reasoning that draws on relevant knowledge and understanding. *Clear reference to religion.*	7–9 marks
2	One point of view developed through a logical chain of reasoning that draws on relevant knowledge and understanding

OR Two different points of view with supporting reasons. *Students cannot move above Level 2 if they don't include a reference to religion, or only give one viewpoint.* | 4–6 marks |
| 1 | One point of view with supporting reasons

OR Two different points of view, simply expressed. | 1–3 marks |

TIP

This question is worth the same amount of marks as the 1, 2, 4 and 5 mark questions combined. Try to aim for at least a full page of writing, and spend 12 minutes or more on this question.

Tips for answering the 12 mark question

- **Remember to focus your answer on the statement you've been given**, for example 'War is never right.'

- **Include different viewpoints, one supporting the statement, one arguing against it** – for example one viewpoint to support the idea that war is *never* right, and an alternative viewpoint to suggest that war is sometimes necessary.

- **Develop both arguments showing a logical chain of reasoning** – draw widely on your knowledge and understanding of the subject of war, try to make **connections** between ideas. Write a detailed answer and use evidence to support your arguments.

- **Be sure to include religious arguments** – a top level answer will explain how religious teaching is relevant to the argument.

- **Include evaluation** – you can make judgements on the strength of arguments throughout, and you should finish with a justified conclusion. If you want to, you can give your own opinion.

- **Write persuasively** – **use a minimum of three paragraphs** (one giving arguments for the statement, one for a different point of view and a final conclusion). The examiner will expect to see extended writing and full sentences.

Spelling, punctuation and grammar

Additional marks for **SPaG – spelling, punctuation and grammar** will be awarded on the 12 mark question.

A maximum of 3 marks will be awarded if:

* your spelling and punctuation are consistently accurate

* you use grammar properly to control the meaning of what you are trying to say

* you use specialist and religious terminology appropriately. For example, the examiner will be impressed if you use appropriately the term 'resurrection' rather than just 'rising from the dead'.

In Paper 1, SPaG will be awarded on the Beliefs question for each religion.

In Paper 2, SPaG will be assessed on each 12 mark question, and the examiner will pick your best mark to add to the total.

> **TIP**
>
> Always try to use your best written English in the long 12 mark questions. It could be a chance to pick up extra marks for SPaG.

How to revise using this book

This Revision Guide takes a three step approach to help with your revision.

RECAP	This is an overview of the key information. It is not a substitute for the full student book, or your class notes. It should prompt you to recall more in-depth information. Diagrams and images are included to help make the information more memorable.
APPLY	Once you've recapped the key information, you can practise applying it to help embed the information. There are two questions after each Recap section. The first question will help you rehearse some key skills that you need for the questions on the exam that test your knowledge (the 1, 2, 4 and 5 mark questions). The second question will help you rehearse some key skills that you will need for the 12 mark question, which tests your evaluative skills. There are suggested answers to the Apply activities at the back of the book.
REVIEW	At the end of each chapter you will then have a chance to review what you've revised. The exam practice pages contain exam-style questions for each question type. For the 4, 5 and 12 mark questions, there are writing frames that you can use to structure your answer, and to remind yourself of what it is that the examiner is looking for. When you've answered the questions you can use the mark schemes at the back of the book to see how you've done. You might identify some areas that you need to revise in more detail. And you can turn back to the pages here for guidance on how to answer the exam questions.

The revision guide is designed so that alongside revising *what* you need to know, you can practise *how* to apply this knowledge in your exam. There are regular opportunities to try out exam practice questions, and mark schemes so you can see how you are doing. Keep recapping, applying and reviewing, particularly going over those areas that you feel unsure about, and hopefully you will build in skills and confidence for the final exam.

Good luck!

1.1 The nature of God

RECAP

Essential information:

☐ Christianity is the main religion in Great Britain.

☐ Christianity has three main traditions: Catholic, Protestant and Orthodox.

☐ Christianity is **monotheistic**, meaning that Christians believe in one Supreme Being, **God**.

Different branches of Christianity

CHRISTIANITY

Catholic – based in Rome and led by the Pope.

Orthodox – split from Catholic Christianity in 1054 CE and practised in Eastern Europe.

Protestant – split from Catholic Christianity in the 16th century and branched out into different **denominations** (distinct groups), e.g. Baptist, Pentecostal, Methodist, United Reformed Churches. Protestants agree that the Bible is the only authority for Christians.

TIP

If you are asked about similarities and differences in a religion, try to remember that even though Christianity has different denominations, they all share the same belief in God.

What do Christians believe about God?

- There is only one God:

> ❝ We believe in one God ❞
> *The Nicene Creed*

- God is the creator and sustainer of all that exists.
- God works throughout history and inspires people to do God's will.
- People can have a relationship with God through prayer.
- God is spirit (John 4:24) – neither male nor female – but has qualities of both.
- God is **holy** (set apart for a special purpose and worthy of worship).
- Jesus is God's son – the true representation of God on earth (Hebrews 1:3).

TIP

See page 13 for more Christian beliefs about God.

APPLY

A Christians believe that there is only one God. Refer to scripture or another Christian source of authority to support this idea.

B 'Christianity is a major influence on people's lives.'

Write a paragraph to **support this statement**.

Essential information:

Christians believe:

☐ God is **omnipotent**, almighty, having unlimited power.

☐ God is **benevolent**, all-loving and all-good.

☐ God is **just**, the perfect judge of human behaviour who will bring about what is right and fair or who will make up for a wrong that has been committed.

Some qualities of God

Omnipotent	Benevolent	Just
• God is the Supreme Being who is all-powerful. • God has unlimited authority.	• God uses his power to do good. • God shows his love by creating humans and caring for them. • God showed his love by sending God's Son, Jesus, to earth.	• God is a just judge of humankind. • God will never support injustice, ill-treatment, prejudice or oppression.

The problems of evil and suffering

The problems of evil and suffering challenge belief in these qualities of God:

- If God is benevolent, **why does God allow people to suffer**, and to hurt others?
- If God is omnipotent, **why does God not prevent evil and suffering**, such as the suffering caused by natural disasters?
- If God is just, **why does God allow injustice** to take place?

Christians believe a just God treats people fairly, so they trust God even when things seem to be going wrong.

> **TIP**
> See page 73 for more arguments in response to these challenges to belief in God.

See page 73 for more arguments in response to these challenges to belief in God.

APPLY

A Give **two** ways in which Christians believe God shows his benevolence.

B Write the response a Christian would make to someone who said that a loving God would not allow suffering. Think of **two** arguments and develop them.

> **TIP**
> In the 12 mark exam answer, using the key terms 'omnipotent', 'benevolent' and 'just' where appropriate, and spelling them correctly, may gain you more marks for SPaG.

RECAP

Essential information:

- [ ] Christians believe there are three persons in the one God: Father, Son and Holy Spirit. This belief is called the **Trinity**.
- [ ] Each person of the Trinity is fully God.
- [ ] The persons of the Trinity are not the same.

TIP

The Apostles Creed and/or the Nicene Creed, Christian statements of belief, are useful to know when discussing the Trinity. They begin 'I/We believe in one God' and include references to 'the Father Almighty', 'the Son' and 'the Holy Spirit'.

The Trinity

- God is understood by Christians as a relationship of love between Father, Son and Holy Spirit.
- In describing God as Trinity, 'person' does not mean a physical being, although Jesus did have a physical presence in history.

God the Father, the creator of all life, acts as a good father towards his children. He is all powerful (omnipotent), all loving (omnibenevolent), all knowing (omniscient) and present everywhere (omnipresent).

God the Son became incarnate through Jesus who was both fully human while on earth and fully God at all times. Jesus is called the **Son of God** to show his special relationship to God the Father.

God the Holy Spirit is the unseen power of God at work in the world, who influences, guides and sustains life on earth.

APPLY

A Here are **two** Christian beliefs about the Trinity. Develop each point with further explanation or a relevant quotation:

1. *"The Trinity is the Christian belief that there are three persons in the one God."* _____
   _____

2. *"One of the persons of the Trinity is God the Father."* _____
   _____

B Here are some arguments that could be used to evaluate the statement, 'The Trinity is a helpful way of describing God.' Sort them into arguments in support of the statement, and arguments in support of different views. **Write your own justified conclusion.**

1. The Trinity is a helpful idea because it describes God as a loving relationship of persons.	5. If God is One, then how can God have three persons?
2. The love of God the Son is shown in Jesus' mission and sacrifice.	6. The Holy Spirit is the outpouring of love between Father and Son that encourages Christians to love their neighbour.
3. The Trinity seems contradictory.	7. Jesus was a Jew and believed in the oneness of God.
4. The love of God the Father is shown in his sending his Son to earth to save humankind.	8. The Trinity is not helpful to people of other faiths as they may think that Christians believe in three different Gods.

1.4 Different Christian beliefs about Creation

Essential information:

☐ Christians believe in **creation** by God, the act by which God brought the universe into being.

☐ God, the Father, chose to design and create the earth and all life on it.

☐ The Holy Spirit was active in the creation (Genesis 1:1–3).

☐ The **Word**, God the Son or Jesus, was active in the creation (John 1:1–3).

☐ The Trinity, therefore, existed from the beginning and was involved in the creation.

Creation: *Genesis 1:1–3*

> ❝ **In the beginning, God created the heavens and the earth.** Now the earth was formless and empty, darkness was over the surface of the deep, and the Spirit of God was hovering over the waters. And God said, "Let there be light," and there was light. ❞
>
> *Genesis 1: 1–3* [NIV]

- Many Christians believe that the story of the creation in Genesis, while not scientifically accurate, contains religious truth.
- Some Christians believe that God made the world in literally six days.
- God created everything out of choice and created everything 'good'.
- Christians believe that God continues to create new life today.
- Although God the Father is referred to as the creator, the Holy Spirit was active in the creation, according to Genesis.

Creation: *John 1:1-3*

> ❝ In the beginning was the Word, and **the Word was with God, and the Word was God.** He was with God in the beginning. Through him all things were made; without him nothing was made that has been made. ❞
>
> *John 1: 1–3* [NIV]

- In John's gospel, everything was created through the Word, who was both with God and was God.
- The Word refers to the Son of God who entered history as Jesus.
- Christians believe that the Son of God, the Word of God, was involved in the creation.

TIP
See pages 58 and 70–71 for more detail on different Christian beliefs about creation.

(A) Explain **two** ways in which belief in creation by God influences Christians today.

(B) Here is an argument in support of the statement, 'The Bible is the best source of information about the creation.'

Evaluate the argument. Explain your reasoning.

"The Bible contains the truth about the creation of the world by God. God is omnipotent, so God can just say 'Let there be light' and it happens. The Bible is God's word, so it is true. Other theories about the creation, like evolution and the Big Bang theory, have not been proved."

TIP
Show the examiner that you are aware of contrasting views within Christianity about the way Genesis 1 is interpreted, that is, between those who take the story literally and those who do not.

RECAP

Essential information:

☐ Christians believe that Jesus was God in human form, a belief known as the **incarnation** (becoming flesh, taking a human form).

☐ Christians believe that Jesus was the Son of God, one of the persons of the Trinity.

The incarnation

> ❝ This is how the birth of Jesus the Messiah came about: His mother Mary was pledged to be married to Joseph, but before they came together, **she was found to be pregnant through the Holy Spirit.** ❞
>
> *Matthew 1:18* [NIV]

- On separate occasions an angel appeared to Mary and Joseph explaining that it was not an ordinary conception and it was not to be an ordinary child.
- The gospels of Matthew and Luke explain that Mary conceived Jesus without having sex.
- The virgin conception is evidence for the Christian belief that Jesus was the Son of God, part of the Trinity.
- Through the incarnation, God showed himself as a human being (Jesus) for around 30 years.

> ❝ **The Word became flesh** and made his dwelling among us. ❞
>
> *John 1:14* [NIV]

Son of God, Messiah, Christ

- Jesus was fully God and fully human, which helps explain his miracles and **resurrection** (rising from the dead).
- His words, deeds and promises have great authority because they are the word of God.
- Most Jews expected a Messiah who would come to save Israel and establish an age of peace, but do not believe that Jesus was that person.
- Christians believe that Jesus is the Messiah, but a spiritual rather than a political one.
- Gospel writers refer to Jesus as the Christ ('anointed one' or Messiah), but Jesus warned his disciples not to use the term, possibly because his opponents would have him arrested for **blasphemy** (claiming to be God).

Jesus •

'The Word'

Christ

Messiah •

God the Son, one of the persons in the Trinity

Son of God

APPLY

A Explain **two** Christian beliefs about Jesus' incarnation. **Refer to sacred writings in your answer.**

B **Develop this argument** to support the statement, 'The stories of the incarnation show that Jesus was the Son of God' by explaining in more detail, adding an example, or referring to a relevant religious teaching or quotation.

"The stories of the incarnation in the gospels of Matthew and Luke show that his mother, Mary, was a virgin. Joseph was not the natural father of Jesus. Jesus' conception was through the Holy Spirit, so really God was his father. That is why he is called the Son of God."

TIP

In a 5 mark question, you need to give a detailed explanation of each belief and then support your answer by quoting from scripture or sacred writings for full marks. The sacred writings may refer to just one of the beliefs or to both of them.

1.6 The crucifixion

RECAP

Essential information:

- [ ] Jesus was sentenced to death by Pontius Pilate, a death by **crucifixion** (fixed to a cross).
- [ ] Jesus forgave those who crucified him and promised one of the men crucified with him that he would join God in paradise.
- [ ] Jesus' body was buried in a cave-like tomb.

Jesus' crucifixion – what happened?

- Although Jesus was fully God, he was also fully human so suffered pain and horror.
- Jesus' last words before dying were:

> **"** Father, into your hands I commit my spirit. **"**
>
> *Luke 23:46* [NIV]

- A Roman centurion acknowledged Jesus was innocent, and said he was the Son of God (Mark 15:39).
- The Roman guards made sure Jesus was dead.
- Joseph of Arimathea was permitted to bury Jesus in a cave-like tomb, rolling a large stone to block the entrance.
- Jesus' burial was rushed because the Sabbath was about to begin.

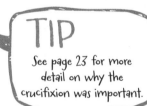

Jesus' crucifixion – why is it important?

- Jesus' sacrifice on the cross gives hope to Christians that **their sins will be forgiven if they sincerely repent**.
- Christians believe that **God understands human suffering** because Jesus, who is God, experienced it.
- **Christians accept that suffering is part of life**, just as it was a part of Jesus' life.

> **TIP**
>
> See page 23 for more detail on why the crucifixion was important.

APPLY

A Here are two ways in which Jesus' crucifixion influences Christians today:

1) *Their sins are forgiven.*
2) *They have hope when they are suffering.*

Develop both points by **explaining in more detail or by adding an example**.

> **TIP**
>
> Keep rereading the statement to make sure you are answering the question asked.

B Read the following response to the statement, 'The crucifixion is the most important belief for Christians.' Underline the **two** best arguments. Explain how this answer could be improved.

"Jesus was arrested in the Garden of Gethsemane and brought to trial, first before the Jewish Council and then before the Roman Governor, Pontius Pilate. In the gospels it says that Pontius Pilate did not think Jesus was guilty of anything, so he didn't want to have him killed. Instead he had him flogged. The Jewish leaders called for Jesus' death, so Pilate gave in to their wishes and sentenced Jesus to death. After about six hours of agony on the cross, Jesus died. A Roman centurion said that because Jesus was innocent, he must surely be the Son of God. When Jesus died, he took the sins of everyone on himself. This is called the atonement. If Jesus had not died, he would not have risen from the dead."

RECAP

Essential information:

- [ ] The gospels say that after Jesus died and was buried, he rose from the dead. This event is known as the **resurrection**.
- [ ] The **ascension** of Jesus took place 40 days after his resurrection, when he returned to God the Father in **heaven**.
- [ ] There would be no Christian faith without the resurrection.

The resurrection of Jesus – what happened?

- Early on Sunday morning, some of Jesus' female followers, including Mary Magdalene, visited the tomb to anoint Jesus' body.
- Jesus' body was not there.
- Either a man or two men, who may have been angels, told the women to spread the news that Jesus had risen from the dead.
- Over the next few days, Jesus appeared to several people including Mary Magdalene and his disciples. He told them he had risen from the dead, as he predicted he would before the crucifixion.

> **"** And if Christ has not been raised, our preaching is useless and so is your faith. But Christ has indeed been raised from the dead… For as in Adam all die, so in Christ all will be made alive. **"**
>
> *1 Corinthians 15:14, 20, 22 [NIV]*

TIP

This quote shows that Christianity would not exist without the resurrection. It also shows that the resurrection is important because it is significant evidence for Christians of the divine nature of Jesus.

The ascension of Jesus – what happened?

- After meeting with his disciples and asking them to carry on his work, Jesus left them for the last time, returning to the Father in heaven. This event is called the ascension.

> **"** While he was blessing them, he left them and was taken up into heaven. **"**   *Luke 24:51 [NIV]*

The significance of these events for Christians today

The significance of the **resurrection**:	The significance of the **ascension**:
• Shows the power of good over evil and life over death. • Means Christians' sins will be forgiven if they follow God's laws. • Means Christians will be resurrected if they accept Jesus, so there is no need to fear death.	• Shows Jesus is with God in heaven. • Paves the way for God to send the Holy Spirit to provide comfort and guidance.

APPLY

(A) Give **two** reasons why the disciples believed Jesus was alive after his resurrection. (AQA Specimen question paper, 2017)

(B) 'The resurrection is the most important belief for Christians.'

Develop this response to the statement, by adding a relevant religious teaching or quotation.

"Without the resurrection, there would be no Christian faith. Jesus' death would have been the end of all the hopes the disciples placed on him. He would have been just like all the other innocent victims put to death for their beliefs."

1.8 Resurrection and life after death

Essential information:

- [ ] Jesus' resurrection assures Christians that they too will rise and live on after death.
- [ ] Christians have differing views about what happens when a person who has died is resurrected.
- [ ] Belief in resurrection affects the way Christians live their lives today.

Different Christian views about resurrection

Some Christians believe a person's soul is resurrected **soon after death**.	Other Christians believe the dead will be resurrected at **some time in the future**, when Jesus will return to judge everyone who has ever lived.
Catholic and Orthodox Christians believe in bodily resurrection. This means resurrection is **both spiritual and physical**: the physical body lost at death is restored and transformed into a new, spiritual body.	Some other Christians believe resurrection will **just be spiritual**, not physical as well.

> **❝** So will it be with the resurrection of the dead. The body that is sown is perishable, it is raised imperishable; it is sown in dishonour, it is raised in glory; it is sown in weakness, it is raised in power; it is sown a natural body, it is raised a spiritual body. If there is a natural body, there is also a spiritual body. **❞**
>
> 1 Corinthians 15:42–44 [NIV]

TIP

This quote explains some of the differences between a living body and a resurrected body. For Catholics and Orthodox Christians, it suggests there is a physical element to resurrection, as it talks about the resurrected body being a 'body', even if it is a spiritual one.

Impact of the belief in resurrection

- inspires Christians to live life in the way God wants them to, so they can remain in his presence in this life and the next
- means life after death is real
- gives hope of a future life with Jesus

A belief in resurrection...

- shows Christians how much God loves them
- gives confidence in the face of death

A Explain **two** ways in which a belief in resurrection influences Christians today.

B The table below presents arguments for and against the belief in bodily resurrection. **Write a paragraph** to explain whether you agree or disagree with bodily resurrection, having evaluated both sides of the argument.

TIP

If you need to give different points of view in your answer to an evaluation question, you could include contrasting non-religious perspectives as well as religious perspectives.

For	Against
Jesus rose from the dead and appeared to his disciples.	Science has shown the body decays after death, so there cannot be a physical resurrection.
The gospels insist he was not a ghost, as he ate with them and showed his wounds to them.	Some people are cremated so their bodies no longer exist.
Yet he could appear and disappear suddenly, so it seems that his body was transformed.	Stories of the resurrection appearances may have been exaggerated.
Paul says 'the body that is sown is perishable, it is raised imperishable', suggesting the natural body is raised as a spiritual body, but a body nevertheless.	The disciples may have felt Jesus' presence spiritually rather than seeing him physically.
Catholic and Orthodox Christians believe people's bodies are transformed into a glorified state in which suffering will not exist.	Christians believe in the soul and it is the soul that rises again, not the body.

RECAP

Essential information:

- ☐ Christians believe in an **afterlife** (life after death) that depends on faith in God.
- ☐ The afterlife begins at death or at the **Day of Judgement**, when Jesus will come to judge the living and the dead.
- ☐ Judgement will be based on how people have behaved during their lifetimes, as well as their faith in following Jesus. This has an effect on how Christians choose to live their lives today.

The afterlife

Christian beliefs about life after death vary, but many believe that:

- They will be **resurrected** and receive **eternal life** after they die.
- This is a gift from God, and **dependent on faith** in God.
- They will be **judged by God** at some point after they die, and either rewarded by being sent to heaven or punished by being sent to hell.
- This judgement will happen either **very soon after death** or **on the Day of Judgement**. This is a time in the future when the world will end and Christ will come again to judge the living and the dead.

Some of these beliefs about the afterlife are found in the **Apostles' Creed**, which is an important statement of Christian faith:

> ❝ He ascended into heaven, and is seated at the right hand of the Father,
> and he will come to judge the living and the dead:
> I believe in…
> the resurrection of the body;
> and the life everlasting. ❞
>
> *The Apostles' Creed*

Judgement

- Christians believe that after they die, God will judge them on their **behaviour and actions** during their lifetime, as well as their **faith in Jesus** as God's Son.
- In the Bible, Jesus' **parable of the Sheep and the Goats** describes how God will judge people.
- This parable teaches Christians that **in serving others**, **they are serving Jesus**, so this is the way they should live their lives.

> ❝ For I was hungry and you gave me something to eat, I was thirsty and you gave me something to drink, I was a stranger and you invited me in, I needed clothes and you clothed me, I was ill and you looked after me, I was in prison and you came to visit me. ❞
>
> *Matthew 25:35–36* [NIV]

- Before he died, Jesus told his disciples he would prepare a place for them in heaven with God. He also made it clear that **having faith in him and following his teachings** was essential for being able to enter heaven when he said:

> ❝ I am the way and the truth and the life. No one comes to the Father except through me. ❞   *John 14:6* [NIV]

APPLY

(A) Explain **two** Christian teachings about judgement. **Refer to sacred writings or another source of Christian belief and teaching in your answer.**
(AQA Specimen question paper, 2017)

(B) **Evaluate the statement**, 'The afterlife is a good way to get people to behave themselves and help others.' Refer to two developed Christian arguments, and two developed non-religious arguments. **Write a justified conclusion.**

TIP

When writing a justified conclusion, do not just repeat everything you have already said. Instead, weigh up the arguments and come to a personal view about their persuasiveness.

Essential information:

☐ Many Christians believe God's judgement will result in eternal reward or eternal punishment.

☐ **Heaven** is the state or place of eternal happiness and peace in the presence of God.

☐ **Hell** is the place of eternal suffering or the state of being without God.

What happens after God's judgement?

- After God's judgement, Christians believe they will either **experience eternal happiness in the presence of God** (heaven), or **be unable to experience God's presence** (hell).
- Catholics believe some people might enter an intermediate state, called purgatory, before they enter heaven.
- Knowledge of these states is limited and linked to imagery from the past.

Heaven and purgatory

- **Heaven** is thought to be either a **physical place** or **spiritual state** of peace, joy, freedom from pain and a chance to be with loved ones.
- Traditional images of heaven often show God on a throne with Jesus next to him and angels all around him, or a garden paradise.
- Christians differ in their views about **who is allowed into heaven**, where there may be:
  - only Christians (believers in Jesus)
  - Christians and other religious people who have pleased God by living good lives
  - baptised Christians, regardless of how they lived their lives.
- However, many Christians believe heaven is a reward for **both faith and actions** – not just one of these – as the parable of the Sheep and the Goats seems to show (see page 20).
- **Purgatory** is an intermediate state where souls are cleansed in order to enter heaven. This is a Catholic belief.

Hell

- **Hell** is seen as the opposite of heaven – a state of existence without God.
- It is often pictured as a **place of eternal torment** in a fiery pit ruled by Satan (a name for the Devil), who is the power and source of evil.
- However, many people question whether a loving God would condemn people to eternal torment and pain in hell.
- Christians who believe God would not do this see hell as an **eternal state of mind** of **being cut off from the possibility of God**.
- Hell would then be what awaits someone who did not acknowledge God or follow his teachings during their life.

(A) Give **two** reasons why some people do not believe in hell.

(B) **Make a list of arguments** for and against the idea that heaven and hell were invented to encourage people to behave themselves.

TIP
If this question said 'some Christians', you should offer Christian objections to the idea of hell. 'Some people' means you can give non-religious reasons if you wish.

RECAP

Essential information:

☐ **Sin** is any thought or action that separates humans from God.

☐ **Original sin** is the in-built tendency to do wrong and disobey God, which Catholics believe all people are born with.

☐ The ways Christians can be saved from sin to gain salvation include following God's **law**, receiving God's **grace**, and being guided by the **Holy Spirit**.

The origins and meanings of sin

A sin is any **thought or action that separates humans from God**. Sinful thoughts (such as anger) can lead to sinful actions (such as murder).

- Some sins, like murder or assault, are illegal.
- Other sins, like adultery, are not illegal but are against the laws of God.

Christians believe that all humans commit sins. Some Christians (particularly Catholics) also believe humans are born with an in-built tendency to sin, called **original sin**.

- The idea of original sin comes from Adam and Eve's disobedience of God, when they ate the fruit of the tree of knowledge of good and evil which was forbidden by God. This was the first (original) sin.
- The result of their sin was separation from God, and the introduction of death into the world.

Christians believe **God gave people free will**, but they should use their freedom to make choices God would approve of, otherwise they will separate themselves from God. God provides people with the guidance to make good choices in his law, for example the Ten Commandments (Exodus 20:1–19), the Beatitudes (Matthew 5:1–12) and other Christian teachings.

Salvation

- **Salvation** means to be saved from sin and its consequences, and to be granted eternal life with God.
- Salvation **repairs the damage caused by sin**, which has separated people from God.

There are two main Christian ideas about how salvation can come about:

- Through **doing good works** – the Old Testament makes it clear that salvation comes through faith in God and obeying God's law.

> **❝**In the same way, faith by itself, if it is not accompanied by action, is dead. **❞**
>
> *James 2:17* [NIV]

- Through **grace** – salvation is given freely by God through faith in Jesus. It is not deserved or earned, but is a free gift of God's love.

> **❝**For it is by grace you have been saved... **❞**
>
> *Ephesians 2:8* [NIV]

- Christians believe it is the **Holy Spirit** who gives grace to Christians and continues to guide them in their daily lives, to help them achieve salvation.

APPLY

(A) Explain **two** Christian teachings about the means of salvation. **Refer to sacred writings or another source of Christian belief and teaching in your answer.** (AQA Specimen question paper, 2017)

(B) 'As nobody is perfect, it is impossible not to sin.' **Evaluate this argument** and explain your reasoning.

"It is perfectly possible to live a good life without sin. Jesus lived his life without sin. Many saints have lived good and courageous lives without acting badly to other people. It is true that nobody is totally perfect, but that's different. Sin separates you from God and goes against God's law, and there are many people who stay close to God and keep his commandments, so I disagree with the statement."

Essential information:

☐ Christians believe that salvation is offered through the life and teaching of Jesus.

☐ Jesus' resurrection shows that God accepted Jesus' sacrifice as **atonement**. This means that through the sacrifice of his death, Jesus restored the relationship between God and humanity that was broken when Adam and Eve sinned.

The role of Jesus in salvation

Christians believe Jesus' life, death and resurrection had a crucial role to play in God's plan for salvation because:

- Jesus' crucifixion **made up for the original sin** of Adam and Eve.
- The death of Jesus, as an innocent man, was necessary to **restore the relationship between God and believers**, to bring them salvation.
- Jesus' resurrection shows the goodness of Jesus defeated the evil of sin. It was proof that God had accepted Jesus' sacrifice on behalf of humankind.
- Jesus' resurrection means humans can now receive forgiveness for their sins.
- Jesus' death and resurrection made it possible for all who follow his teachings to **gain eternal life**.

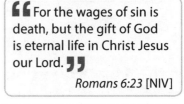

> **TIP**
> This quote shows the Christian belief that death came into the world as a punishment for sin, but salvation is offered through the life and teaching of Jesus.

> ❝For the wages of sin is death, but the gift of God is eternal life in Christ Jesus our Lord. ❞
> *Romans 6:23* [NIV]

Atonement

- Atonement **removes the effects of sin** and allows people to restore their relationship with God.
- Many Christians believe that through the sacrifice of his death, Jesus took the sins of all humanity on himself and paid the debt for them all. He **atoned for the sins of humanity**.
- This sacrifice makes it possible for all who follow Jesus' teachings to **receive eternal life** with God.

> ❝[…] if anybody does sin, we have an advocate with the Father – Jesus Christ, the Righteous One. He is the atoning sacrifice for our sins, and not only for ours but also for the sins of the whole world. ❞ *1 John 2:1–2* [NIV]

Jesus' death + grace and good works

sin   atonement

A Give **two** reasons why the death and resurrection of Jesus is important to Christians.

B Here are some sentences that could be used to evaluate the statement, 'Salvation is God's greatest gift to humans.'

Sort them into arguments in support of the statement, and arguments in support of different views. Try to put them in a logical order. What do you think is missing from these statements to make a top level answer? Explain how the answer could be improved.

> **TIP**
> To remember the meaning of 'atonement', think of it as 'at-one-ment', because Jesus' death and resurrection make people at one with God.

1. Atheists do not consider salvation important because they do not think there is a God who saves people.	5. Without salvation, humankind would have to pay the price of human sin.
2. God shows his great love for people by sending his Son to save us.	6. People may doubt the truth of Jesus' resurrection so they don't see the need for a belief in salvation.
3. Even some religious people may think there are greater gifts to humans, such as nature or life itself.	7. Some people may question whether God is loving if God demands the death of his Son in payment for human sin.
4. Everyone needs forgiveness from God.	8. Humans should be grateful every day of their lives for Jesus' sacrifice on their behalf.

Test the 1 mark question

1. Which **one** of the following is the idea that God became human in Jesus?

   A Atonement   B Incarnation   C Resurrection   D Creation   **[1 mark]**

2. Which **one** of the following is the idea that God is loving?

   A Omniscient   B Omnipotent   C Benevolent   D Immanent   **[1 mark]**

Test the 2 mark question

3. Give **two** ways that Christians believe salvation can come about.   **[2 marks]**

   1) _____

   2) _____

4. Give **two** Christian beliefs about life after death.   **[2 marks]**

   1) _____

   2) _____

Test the 4 mark question

5. Explain **two** ways in which a belief in Jesus' crucifixion influences Christians today.   **[4 marks]**

● **Explain one way.**	*One way in which a belief in Jesus' crucifixion influences Christians today is that they believe that the crucifixion was a sacrifice Jesus chose to make for them*
● Develop your explanation with more detail/an example/ reference to a religious teaching or quotation.	*in order to give them the opportunity to be granted forgiveness by God, so they can live in confidence that their sins have been forgiven.*
● **Explain a second way.**	*A second way in which a belief in Jesus' crucifixion influences Christians today is that it helps Christians who are suffering because they know Jesus suffered as well.*
● Develop your explanation with more detail/an example/ reference to a religious teaching or quotation.	*For example, Christians who are suffering persecution for their faith will be comforted to know that Jesus understands what they are going through because he too was innocent and suffered for his beliefs.*

6. Explain **two** ways in which the belief in creation by God influences Christians today.   **[4 marks]**

● **Explain one way.**	
● Develop your explanation with more detail/an example/ reference to a religious teaching or quotation.	
● **Explain a second way.**	
● Develop your explanation with more detail/an example/ reference to a religious teaching or quotation.	

TIP

The student has explained the influence a belief in Jesus' crucifixion has on a Christian's <u>attitude</u> (their confidence in being forgiven and their comfort in dealing with their own suffering). You could also discuss the influence of this belief on a Christian's <u>life</u> (e.g. it might encourage them to spread the message of Jesus or to make the sign of the cross when they pray to remind themselves of Jesus' sacrifice).

7. Explain **two** ways in which the belief that God is loving influences Christians today.   **[4 marks]**

1 Exam practice

Test the 5 mark question

8 Explain **two** Christian beliefs about salvation.

Refer to sacred writings or another source of Christian belief and teaching in your answer. **[5 marks]**

● **Explain one belief.**	One Christian belief about salvation is that salvation can be gained through good works.
● Develop your explanation with more detail/an example.	These good works may be following teachings such as the Ten Commandments, the Golden Rule and 'love your neighbour'. Worshipping and praying regularly also help Christians to earn salvation.
● **Explain a second belief.**	A second Christian belief about salvation is that it is gained through grace.
● Develop your explanation with more detail/an example.	God gives salvation to people who have faith in Jesus. It is a gift for the faithful.
● Add a reference to sacred writings or another source of Christian belief and teaching. If you prefer, you can add this reference to your first belief instead.	Paul wrote in his letters that it is through grace, which is a gift from God, that people are saved, not simply through their good works.

TIP
The references to scripture here count as development of your first point.

9 Explain **two** Christian teachings about God.

Refer to sacred writings or another source of Christian belief and teaching in your answer. **[5 marks]**

● **Explain one teaching.**	
● Develop your explanation with more detail/an example.	
● **Explain a second teaching.**	
● Develop your explanation with more detail/an example.	
● Add a reference to sacred writings or another source of Christian belief and teaching. If you prefer, you can add this reference to your first teaching instead.	

TIP
You only need to make one reference to scripture in your answer. It can support either your first or your second point.

10 Explain **two** Christian teachings about atonement.

Refer to sacred writings or another source of Christian belief and teaching in your answer. **[5 marks]**

Test the 12 mark question

11 'The stories of the incarnation prove that Jesus was the Son of God.'

Evaluate this statement. In your answer you should:

- refer to Christian teaching
- give reasoned arguments to support this statement
- give reasoned arguments to support a different point of view
- reach a justified conclusion.

[12 marks
Plus SPaG 3 ma

REASONED ARGUMENTS IN SUPPORT OF THE STATEMENT ● **Explain why some people would agree with the statement.** ● Develop your explanation with more detail and examples. ● Refer to religious teaching. Use a quote or paraphrase or refer to a religious authority. ● **Evaluate the arguments.** Is this a good argument or not? Explain why you think this.	*Christians believe in the incarnation. This means that God took human form in Jesus. The stories of Jesus' birth show he was not conceived in the normal way. The fact he was conceived through the actions of God and born of a virgin proves that he was special and if God was involved it is likely that Jesus was his son. However, even though he was a physical person, he was also God at the same time. John's gospel calls Jesus 'the Son of God' and says he was the Word made flesh, living among us. This supports the idea that Jesus was both God and human.*
REASONED ARGUMENTS SUPPORTING A DIFFERENT VIEW ● **Explain why some people would support a different view.** ● Develop your explanation with more detail and examples. ● Refer to religious teaching. Use a quote or paraphrase or refer to a religious authority. ● **Evaluate the arguments.** Is this a good argument or not? Explain why you think this.	*Many people do not agree that Jesus was conceived through the actions of God and believe that Mary, his mother, was not a virgin. If the stories of the incarnation are not correct, they cannot be used as evidence that Jesus was the Son of God although his actions showed he was very special.*
CONCLUSION ● **Give a justified conclusion.** ● Include your own opinion together with your own reasoning. ● **Include evaluation.** Explain why you think one viewpoint is stronger than the other or why they are equally strong. ● Do not just repeat arguments you have already used without explaining how they apply to your reasoned opinion/conclusion.	*It may be true that the title 'Son of God' does not mean that there is such a close relationship between Jesus and God. It is possible that he was chosen by God, maybe when he was baptised, to do good works on earth and tell people about Christianity without there being a family relationship between himself and God. If this is true, there is no such thing as incarnation as far as Jesus is concerned.*

TIP

The question is about stories (plural) so it would improve the answer to mention details of Jesus' conception in the gospels of Matthew and Luke.

TIP

This argument could be developed further for more marks. For example, after the sentence that ends 'not a virgin' you might add 'Mary was engaged to Joseph, making it possible that Joseph was Jesus' father.'

TIP

The conclusion shows logical chains of reasoning. It evaluates different interpretations of the title 'Son of God' in relation to the stories of the incarnation. The examiner will want to see that you can link ideas together when developing your argument, and not just repeat what you have said already.

1 Exam practice

12 'There is no such place as hell.'

Evaluate this statement. In your answer you should:

- refer to Christian teaching
- give reasoned arguments to support this statement
- give reasoned arguments to support a different point of view
- reach a justified conclusion.

TIP

Spelling, punctuation and grammar is assessed on each 12 mark question, so make sure you are careful to use your best written English.

[12 marks]

Plus SPaG 3 marks

REASONED ARGUMENTS IN SUPPORT OF THE STATEMENT ● **Explain why some people would agree with the statement.** ● Develop your explanation with more detail and examples. ● Refer to religious teaching. Use a quote or paraphrase or refer to a religious authority. ● **Evaluate the arguments.** Is this a good argument or not? Explain why you think this.	
REASONED ARGUMENTS SUPPORTING A DIFFERENT VIEW ● **Explain why some people would support a different view.** ● Develop your explanation with more detail and examples. ● Refer to religious teaching. Use a quote or paraphrase or refer to a religious authority. ● **Evaluate the arguments.** Is this a good argument or not? Explain why you think this.	
CONCLUSION ● **Give a justified conclusion.** ● Include your own opinion together with your own reasoning. ● **Include evaluation.** Explain why you think one viewpoint is stronger than the other or why they are equally strong. ● Do not just repeat arguments you have already used without explaining how they apply to your reasoned opinion/conclusion.	

TIP

It's essential to include evaluation because this is the key skill that you are being tested on in the 12 mark question. You can evaluate after each viewpoint, and/or at the end as part of your justified conclusion.

13 'The best way to gain salvation is to obey God's law.'

Evaluate this statement. In your answer you should:

- refer to Christian teaching
- give reasoned arguments to support this statement
- give reasoned arguments to support a different point of view
- reach a justified conclusion.

[12 marks]

Plus SPaG 3 marks

Check your answers using the mark scheme on page 121. How did you do?
To feel more secure in the content you need to remember, re-read pages 12–23.
To remind yourself of what the examiner is looking for, go to pages 6–11.

2.1 Worship

RECAP

Essential information:

☐ **Worship** is the act of religious praise, honour or devotion. It is a way for Christians to show their deep love and honour to God.

☐ Worship can take different forms, including liturgical, non-liturgical and informal worship.

☐ **Private worship** is when believers praise or honour God in their own home.

Why do Christians worship?

| To praise and thank God | To ask for forgiveness | To seek God's help for themselves or others | To deepen their relationship with God and strengthen their faith |

Different forms of worship

Type of worship	What form does it take?	Examples	Why is it important for Christians?
liturgical worship is a church service that follows a set structure or ritual	• takes place in a church • priest leads the congregation and may perform symbolic actions • formal prayers with set responses • Bible passages are read out, there may be a sermon • music and hymns	the Eucharist for Catholic, Orthodox and Anglican Churches	• worldwide set order for service that is familiar to everyone • ritual passed down through generations gives a sense of tradition • Bible readings follow the Christian calendar and teach Christian history and faith
non-liturgical worship is a service that does not follow a set text or ritual	• takes place in a church • often focused on Bible readings followed by a sermon • may also have prayers and hymns but there is no set order, the number and type can change from week to week	services in non-Conformist churches, e.g. Methodist, Baptist, United Reformed	• services can be planned and ordered to suit a certain theme • non-Conformist churches place an emphasis on the word of God in the Bible
informal worship is a type of non-liturgical worship that is 'spontaneous' or 'charismatic' in nature	• community or house churches meet in private homes and share food • Quaker worship is mainly silent, people speak when moved by God to offer their thoughts or read from the Bible • 'charismatic' worship may involve dancing, clapping, calling out and speaking in tongues	community or house churches, Quaker worship, charismatic ('led by the spirit') worship of the Pentecostal Church	• the style of worship in house churches is similar to the worship of early Christians • people can share readings and prayers and can take an active part in church by calling out or speaking without formal training • service may have an emotional impact with a feeling of personal revelation from God

APPLY

A Going on pilgrimage, celebrating festivals and religious art are also forms of worship. Give **two** more ways that Christians worship.

B 'Worship is most powerful when believers follow a set ritual.'

List arguments to support this statement and arguments to support a different point of view.

TIP

The arguments should apply to Christianity. Try to use religious language (see key terms in red).

RECAP

Essential information:

- ☐ **Prayer** is communicating with God, either silently or through words of praise, thanksgiving or confession, or requests for God's help or guidance.

- ☐ Christians may use **set prayers** that have been written down and said more than once by more than one person. An example is **the Lord's Prayer**, which is the prayer Jesus taught to his disciples.

- ☐ Christians may also use **informal prayers** (made up by an individual using his or her own words) to communicate with God. Some Christians find they can express their needs to God more easily by using their own words.

The importance of prayer

- encourages reflection in the middle of a busy life
- enables Christians to talk and listen to God
- gives strength in times of trouble
- **Why is prayer important?**
- helps Christians to keep a close relationship with God
- gives a sense of peace
- helps Christians to accept God's will even if it means suffering

The Lord's Prayer

> " Our Father in heaven, hallowed be your name,
> your Kingdom come, your will be done,
> on earth as in heaven.
> Give us today our daily bread.
> Forgive us our sins
> as we forgive those who sin against us.
> Lead us not into temptation, but deliver us from evil.
> For the kingdom, the power, and the glory are yours
> now and for ever. Amen. "
>
> *The Lord's Prayer*

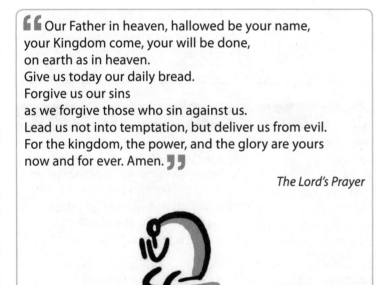

- When Jesus' disciples asked him to teach them how to pray, he answered with the Lord's Prayer.
- Christians see it as a **model of good prayer**, as it combines praise to God with asking for one's needs.
- It reminds Christians to **forgive others in order to be forgiven**, since prayer is only effective if people's relationships with others are right.
- It reminds Christians that **God is the Father of the whole Christian community**, and it can create a sense of unity when everyone in the congregation says it together.
- The Lord's Prayer is often used in worship and is nearly always said at Holy Communion, baptisms, marriages and funerals. It is also used in schools and in commemoration services in Britain.

APPLY

Ⓐ Give **two** reasons why the Lord's Prayer is important to Christians.

Ⓑ 'Private worship has more meaning for a Christian than public worship.' (AQA Specimen question paper, 2017)

Develop this argument to support the statement by explaining in more detail, adding an example, or referring to a relevant religious teaching or quotation.

"An individual Christian can choose how they want to worship in private, whereas in public worship they have to follow what everyone else is saying and doing. Therefore private worship has more meaning because they can put their heart and soul into it."

TIP

Always analyse the statement carefully. For example, here 'has more meaning' might depend on an individual's reasons for prayer.

Essential information:

☐ **Sacraments** are holy rituals through which believers receive a special gift of grace (free gift of God's love). Some Christian denominations recognise seven sacraments while others acknowledge fewer.

☐ **Baptism** is the ritual through which a person becomes a member of the Church. It involves the use of water to symbolise the washing away of sin.

☐ **Infant baptism** is for babies and young children. **Believers' baptism** is for people who are old enough to understand the significance of the ritual.

The sacraments

- **Catholic and Orthodox** Christians recognise **seven** sacraments: baptism, confirmation, Holy Communion, marriage, Holy Orders, reconciliation and the anointing of the sick.
- Many **Protestant** churches recognise **two** sacraments – baptism and Holy Communion – because they believe Jesus taught people to undertake these.
- Some churches that practise believers' baptism consider it to be important but not a 'sacrament'.
- Some churches, like the Quakers or Salvation Army, do not see any ritual or ceremony as being a 'sacrament'.

Baptism

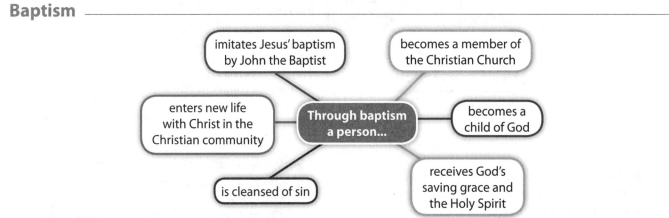

Infant baptism and believers' baptism

	Practised by	Reasons why	What happens
Infant baptism	Catholic, Orthodox, Anglican, Methodist, and United Reformed Christians	• Removes original sin (Catholic and Orthodox belief). • Allows the child to be welcomed into the Church as soon as possible. • The parents can thank God for their new baby and celebrate with family and friends.	• The priest or minister pours blessed water over the baby's head and says, 'I baptise you in the name of the Father, and of the Son, and of the Holy Spirit.' • Godparents and parents promise to bring up the child as a Christian. • The child is welcomed into the Christian community.
Believers' baptism	Baptists, Pentecostalists	• People should be old enough to consciously make a mature decision about their faith. • The decision to live a life dedicated to Jesus is what saves a person, rather than the baptism itself.	• The person is fully immersed in a pool which symbolises cleansing from sin and rising to new life in Christ. • When asked whether they are willing to change their lives, the person gives a brief testimony of their faith in Jesus. • The person is baptised 'in the name of the Father, and of the Son, and of the Holy Spirit.'

Ⓐ Explain **two** contrasting ways in which Christians practise baptism and develop each point.

Ⓑ 'Parents should not have their children baptised if they have no intention of bringing them up as Christians.'

Evaluate this statement.

2.4 The sacraments: Holy Communion

Essential information:

- [ ] **Holy Communion** (also known as the Eucharist) is the sacrament that uses bread and wine to celebrate the sacrifice of Jesus on the cross and his resurrection.
- [ ] It recalls the Last Supper of Jesus, using his words and actions.
- [ ] Christians interpret the meaning of Holy Communion in different ways, but all agree that it brings them closer to each other and to God.

The meaning of Holy Communion

Holy Communion is a service which celebrates and gives thanks for the sacrifice of Jesus' death and resurrection (see pages 17–18). It has different meanings for different Christians:

- **Catholics, Orthodox Christians** and **some Anglicans** believe the bread and wine become **the body and blood of Christ**. This means Jesus is fully present in the bread and wine. This is a divine mystery that helps believers share in the saving sacrifice of Jesus' death and resurrection.
- **Protestant Christians** celebrate Holy Communion as a **reminder of the Last Supper**. They do not believe the bread and wine become the body and blood of Christ. Instead, the bread and wine remain **symbols of Jesus' sacrifice**, which helps believers to reflect on its meaning today.

> " For whenever you eat this bread and drink this cup, you proclaim the Lord's death until he comes. "
>
> *1 Corinthians 11:26 [NIV]*

The impact of Holy Communion

For many Christians, Holy Communion is at the centre of their lives and worship. It affects individuals, local communities and the wider society in a number of ways:

Individuals	Communities	Wider society
• Christians **receive God's grace** by joining in the sacrifice of Jesus. • This helps to strengthen their faith. • They become closer to God.	• Holy Communion **brings the community of believers together** in unity by sharing the bread and wine. • This can provide support and encouragement for those going through a difficult time.	• Holy Communion **acts as a call to love others in practical ways**. • It encourages Christians to work for equality and justice for all. • Many churches collect money during the service to help support those in need, such as the poor or homeless.

A Explain **two** ways in which Holy Communion has an impact on the lives of believers.

B Use the table below with arguments about the statement, 'It is more important to help the poor than to celebrate Holy Communion.'

> **TIP**
>
> Decide on two ways and explain each. Do not simply list a number of ways without developing any of your points.

Write a paragraph to explain whether you agree or disagree with the statement, having evaluated both sides of the argument.

In support of the statement	Other views
The poor need urgent help, particularly if they are living in less economically developed countries, so of course it is more important to help them than to receive Holy Communion. Christians are taught to love their neighbour so that must come before their own needs. Remembering Jesus' death and resurrection through Holy Communion is nice, but not very useful to anyone. It's just focusing on the past when people should be thinking about the present.	It doesn't need to be such a stark choice. After all, when Christians break bread together at Holy Communion they remember that people in the world are starving and they try to help them. Many churches collect money for the poor during the service of Holy Communion, so celebrating this sacrament encourages people to care for others, not just themselves. 'Eucharist' means 'thanksgiving', so it makes Christians grateful for God's love and this makes them want to share it.

RECAP

Essential information:

☐ In most churches the Holy Communion service has two parts: the ministry of the Word (which focuses on the Bible), and the ministry of Holy Communion (the offering, consecrating and sharing of bread and wine).

☐ Christians have different practices when it comes to celebrating Holy Communion.

Differences between Holy Communion services

- In the **Orthodox Church**, Holy Communion is called the Divine Liturgy, and is believed to recreate heaven on earth. Much of the service is held at the altar behind the iconostasis, which is a screen that represents the divide between heaven and earth. The priest passes through the iconostasis using the Royal Doors.
- Holy Communion in the **Catholic and Anglican Churches** is very similar. The main difference is that Catholics believe the bread and wine turn into the body and blood of Christ, whereas many Anglicans believe Jesus is only present in a spiritual way when the bread and wine are being eaten.

Further examples of how Holy Communion services differ from each other include the following:

Orthodox Divine Liturgy	Catholic Mass and Anglican Holy Communion	Holy Communion in the United Reformed Church
Liturgy of the Word: • There are hymns, prayers and a Bible reading. • The priest comes through the Royal Doors to chant the Gospel. • There may be a sermon. **Liturgy of the Faithful:** • The priest receives wine and bread baked by church members. • Prayers are offered for the church, the local community and the world. • Behind the iconostasis, the priest says the words of Jesus at the Last Supper. • Most of the bread is consecrated as the body and blood of Christ. • The priest distributes holy bread and wine on a spoon. • Prayers of thanksgiving are said. • Unconsecrated pieces of bread are given to people to take home, as a sign of belonging to the Christian community.	**Liturgy of the Word:** • There are three Bible readings, a psalm and a homily. • The Creed is said. • Prayers are said for the Church, the local community, the world, and the sick and the dead. **Liturgy of the Eucharist:** • In the Anglican Holy Communion, people give a sign of peace to each other. • Offerings of bread and wine are brought to the altar. • The priest repeats the words of Jesus at the Last Supper over the bread and the wine. • People say the Lord's Prayer. • In the Catholic Mass, the sign of peace is given at this point. • People receive the bread and wine. • The priest blesses people and sends them out to live the gospel.	• The service begins with a hymn and prayer of praise and thanksgiving. • Bible readings and a sermon are given. • Prayers for the world and the needs of particular people are said. • The minister repeats the words and actions of Jesus at the Last Supper. • There is an 'open table' so anyone who wishes may receive Holy Communion. • Sometimes the bread is cut beforehand, other times it is broken and passed around by the congregation. • Wine is sometimes non-alcoholic and is usually distributed in small cups. • The service ends with a prayer of thanksgiving, a blessing, and an encouragement to go out and serve God.

APPLY

A Explain **two** contrasting ways in which Holy Communion is celebrated in Christianity. (AQA Specimen question paper, 2017)

B **Write a paragraph** in response to the statement, 'Holy Communion services should focus more on the Liturgy of the Word than on the Holy Communion itself.' **Develop your reasons** and include a reference to scripture or religious teaching in your answer.

TIP
Holy Communion services have many similarities. Be sure to choose aspects that show a real contrast.

2.6 Pilgrimage

Essential information:

☐ A **pilgrimage** is a journey made by a believer to a holy site for religious reasons. As well as making a physical journey to a sacred place, the pilgrim also makes a spiritual journey towards God.

☐ A pilgrimage gives many opportunities for prayer and worship, and is itself an act of worship and devotion.

☐ Two popular pilgrimage sites for Christians are Lourdes (a town in France) and Iona (a Scottish island).

The role and importance of pilgrimage

- meet others who share the same faith
- experience a holy place
- help other pilgrims who are disabled or ill
- seek a cure for illness
- thank God for a blessing
- **Why go on a pilgrimage?**
- grow closer to God
- strengthen faith in God
- be forgiven for sin
- reflect on one's life
- pray for something special

A pilgrimage can impact on a Christian's life in a number of ways. It can:

- give them a better understanding of their faith
- renew their enthusiasm for living a Christian life
- help them to see problems in a new light
- help them to feel cleansed from sin
- help them to feel more connected to the Christian community
- give them a good feeling about helping other pilgrims who are disabled or ill

Places of Christian pilgrimage

Place	Significance	Activities
Lourdes (a town in France)	• Where Mary is said to have appeared in a number of visions to a young girl called Bernadette. • Mary told Bernadette to dig in the ground, and when she did a spring of water appeared. • The water is believed to have healing properties, and a number of healing miracles are claimed to have taken place here.	• Pilgrims go to Lourdes to bathe in the waters of the spring, or to help other pilgrims who are ill or disabled to bathe in the waters. • Pilgrims also pray for healing or forgiveness. • They may recite the rosary together.
Iona (an island off the coast of Scotland)	• Where St Columba established a monastic community in the 6th century AD. • The community now has an ecumenical centre where pilgrims can stay.	• Because it is quiet, peaceful and a place of natural beauty, pilgrims can spend time praying, reading the Bible, and reflecting or meditating. • Pilgrims can also attend services in the abbey church, take part in workshops, and visit the island's holy or historic sites.

A Explain **two** contrasting examples of Christian pilgrimage. (AQA Specimen question paper, 2017)

B 'There is no difference between a pilgrimage and a holiday.'

Develop this argument against the statement by explaining in more detail, adding an example or referring to Christian teaching.

"Although a pilgrimage can seem a lot like a holiday, especially if you travel abroad, there is a big difference. A pilgrimage is a spiritual journey that people undertake for religious reasons rather than just to sightsee."

TIP
You need to explain why the examples are contrasting, rather than just describing the two places, so be sure to explain the different reasons why pilgrims go there.

RECAP

Essential information:

☐ A **festival** is a day or period of celebration for religious reasons.

☐ Festivals help Christians to remember and celebrate the major events in their religion – particularly the life, death and resurrection of Jesus.

☐ **Christmas** commemorates the incarnation and the birth of Jesus. Celebrations begin on 25 December and last 12 days, ending with Epiphany (which recalls the visit of the wise men).

☐ **Easter** celebrates the resurrection of Jesus from the dead. Celebrations begin before Easter Sunday and finish with the feast of Pentecost.

Christmas

Christmas **commemorates the incarnation of Jesus**, which is the belief that God became human in Jesus (see page 16). The celebrations reflect Christian beliefs and teachings in the following ways:

- **lights** represent Jesus as the light coming into the world of darkness
- **nativity scenes** show baby Jesus born into poverty
- **carol services** with Bible readings remind Christians about God's promise of a saviour and the events of Jesus' birth

- **Midnight Mass** reflects the holiness of the night and the joy Christians feel at Jesus' birth
- **Christmas cards and gifts** recall the wise men's gifts to Jesus
- Christians **give to charity** in this time of peace and goodwill because God gave humanity the gift of Jesus, his Son.

Easter

Easter is the most important Christian festival, which **celebrates Jesus' rising from the dead**.

Holy Week (the week before Easter Sunday) remembers the events leading up to Jesus' crucifixion, including his arrest and trial.

- On **Saturday night**, some churches hold a special service to celebrate Christ's resurrection.
- Orthodox Christians walk with candles in procession, then enter the dark church as if going into Jesus' empty tomb.
- The priest announces 'Christ is risen!' to which people answer 'He is risen indeed.'
- Catholics and Anglicans have a vigil that begins in darkness, before the Paschal candle is lit to symbolise the risen Christ. The service ends with Holy Communion.

On **Good Friday** (the day Jesus was crucified), there are special services and processions led by a person carrying a cross.

- On **Easter Sunday**, churches are filled with flowers and special hymns are sung to rejoice at Jesus' resurrection.
- Services are held at sunrise, and shared breakfasts include eggs to symbolise new life.

> ❝Christ is risen from the dead, trampling down death by death, and upon those in the tombs bestowing life.❞
> *Traditional Orthodox hymn at the Easter Divine Liturgy*

APPLY

A Give **two** ways in which Christians celebrate the festival of Easter.

B 'Christmas is no longer a religious festival.' Evaluate this statement.

2.8 The role of the Church in the local community: Food banks

Essential information:

- **The Church** is the holy people of God, also called the Body of Christ, among whom Christ is present and active.

- **A church** is a building in which Christians worship.

- Individual churches and the Church as a whole help the local community in a variety of ways, including the provision of **food banks**. These give food for free to people who cannot afford to buy it.

What does the Church do?

Individual churches and the Church as a whole help the local community in many ways.

Individual churches:

- educate people about Christianity (e.g. Bible study groups)
- are meeting places for prayer and worship
- provide activities for younger people (e.g. youth clubs)
- are places where Christians can socialise and obtain spiritual guidance.

The Church:

- supports local projects such as food banks
- provides social services such as schooling and medical care
- helps those in need
- campaigns for justice.

> ❝ And God placed all things under his [Jesus'] feet and appointed him to be head over everything for the church, which is his body. ❞
>
> *Ephesians 1:22–23* [NIV]

TIP
You could use this quote in your exam to show that Christians think of the Church as the followers of Jesus, who together are the body of Christ on earth.

Examples of the Church helping the local community

The Trussell Trust and The Oasis Project are two organisations that help the local community by providing food banks and other services. The work of these charities is based on Christian principles (such as the parable of the Sheep and the Goats).

The Trussell Trust
• A charity running over 400 food banks in the UK.
• These provide emergency food, help and support to people in crisis in the UK.
• Non-perishable food is donated by churches, supermarkets, schools, businesses and individuals.
• Doctors, health visitors and social workers identify people in crisis and issue them with a food voucher.
• Their aim is to bring religious and non-religious people together to help end poverty and hunger.

The Oasis Project
• A community hub run by Plymouth Methodist Mission Circuit.
• Provides an internet café, creative courses, a job club, training opportunities, a meeting place and a food bank.
• Spiritual and practical help is given to those in need because of ill health, learning disabilities, domestic violence, substance abuse, low income and housing problems.

TIP
You will not be asked about these particular organisations in your exam, but if you learn what they do, you will be able to give detailed examples of how the Church helps in the local community.

APPLY

A Give **two** meanings of the word 'church'.

B Here is a response to the statement, 'There will always be a need to feed hungry people in Britain.' Can you improve this answer by including religious beliefs?

"At first this statement appears untrue. No one should be hungry in Britain as there is a welfare state. People who can't work to feed themselves or their families can apply for benefits."

"However, I agree with the statement because people can suddenly be faced with bills they can't pay, or lose their jobs, or become ill so they can't work. It may take many weeks to apply for benefits and be accepted, so what do they do in the meantime? If they don't have much savings they will be really hard up and need the help of food banks."

2.9 The role of the Church in the local community: Street Pastors

Essential information:

☐ Christians should help others in the local community because Jesus taught that people should show **agape** love (a Biblical word meaning selfless, sacrificial, unconditional love).

☐ Christians believe it is important to put their faith into action. They do this through many organisations and projects that help vulnerable people in the community.

☐ **Street Pastors** are people who are trained to patrol the streets in urban areas. They help vulnerable people by providing a reassuring presence on the street.

The importance of helping in the local community

- Jesus taught that **Christians should help others by showing agape love** towards them. For example, in the parable of the Sheep and the Goats, Jesus teaches Christians they should give practical help to people in need (see page 20).
- Two examples of Christian organisations that provide practical help to local communities are Street Pastors and Parish Nursing Ministries UK.

> **"** Faith by itself, if it is not accompanied by action, is dead. **"**
>
> *James 2:17* [NIV]

TIP
You could use this quote in your exam to show that Christians believe it is very important to take practical action to help others.

Street Pastors and Parish Nursing Ministries UK

Street Pastors	Parish Nursing Ministries UK
• An initiative started in London in 2003, by the Christian charity the Ascension Trust.	• This Christian charity supports whole-person healthcare through the local church.
• Adult volunteers are trained to patrol the streets in urban areas.	• They provide churches with registered parish nurses, who promote well-being in body, mind and spirit among the local community.
• The main aim originally was to challenge gang culture and knife crime in London.	• The nurses help to provide early diagnosis of health problems.
• The focus then widened to responding to drunkenness, anti-social behaviour and fear of crime.	• They train and coordinate volunteers to help combat loneliness or provide support during times of crisis.
• Street Pastors work closely with police and local councils.	• They give additional help to the NHS.
• They listen to people's problems, advise on where they might get help, and discourage anti-social behaviour.	• They encourage people to exercise and have a good diet.
• A similar group called School Pastors was set up in 2011 to discourage illegal drug use, bullying and anti-social behaviour in schools.	• They focus on the whole person, including listening to people and praying with them if asked. They also direct people to specific services if needed.

TIP
When using Christian charities as examples in your answers, focus on their work and why they do it, rather than details about when they were founded and by whom.

A Explain **two** ways in which Street Pastors carry out their Christian duty.

Refer to Christian teaching in your answer. (AQA Specimen question paper, 2017)

B 'All Christians should do something practical to help their community, including praying for their neighbours.'

Develop two religious arguments in support of this statement, and **two** non-religious arguments against it.

Essential information:

☐ A **mission** is a vocation or calling to spread the faith. The Church has a mission to tell non-believers that Jesus Christ, the Son of God, came into the world as its saviour.

☐ Christians spread the faith through **evangelism** (showing faith in Jesus by example or by telling others).

☐ They do this to fulfil Jesus' instructions to the disciples to spread his teachings (the **Great Commission**).

The Great Commission

> **"** Therefore go and make disciples of all nations, baptising them in the name of the Father and of the Son and of the Holy Spirit, and teaching them to obey everything I have commanded you. **"**
>
> *Matthew 28:19–20* [NIV]

TIP

You can use this quote in your exam to show what the Great Commission involves. Jesus instructs his disciples to baptise people and to spread his teachings.

- Jesus gave a Great Commission to his disciples to **spread the gospel** and **make disciples of all nations through baptism**.
- The **Holy Spirit** at Pentecost gave the disciples the gifts and courage needed to carry out the Great Commission.
- All Christians have a duty to spread the gospel and tell others of their faith, but some become **missionaries** or **evangelists** (people who promote Christianity, for example by going to foreign countries to preach or do charitable work).
- The aims of missionary work and evangelism are to **persuade people to accept Jesus as their Saviour**, and to extend the Church to all nations.

Alpha

- Alpha is an **example of evangelism in Britain**.
- It was started in London by an Anglican priest, with the aim of helping church members understand the basics of the Christian faith.
- The course is now used as an **introduction for those interested in learning about Christianity**, by different Christian denominations in Britain and abroad.
- The organisers describe it as 'an opportunity to explore the meaning of life' through talks and discussions.
- Courses are held in homes, workplaces, universities and prisons as well as in churches.

APPLY

A Give **two** ways in which the Church tries to fulfil its mission.

B **Unscramble the arguments** in the table below referring to the statement, 'Every Christian should be an evangelist.' Decide which arguments could be used to support the statement and which could be used against it.

Write a paragraph to explain whether you agree or disagree with the statement, having evaluated both sides of the argument.

1. If Christians don't help to spread the faith, it might die out.	4. Not every Christian should be an evangelist because some people are just too shy.
2. Some Christians live in countries where they are persecuted, so if they spoke in public about their faith they would be risking death or imprisonment.	5. All Christians have received the Great Commission from Jesus to preach to all nations.
3. Evangelism can happen in small ways, for example Christians can spread their faith to people they meet in everyday life or just give a good example of loving their neighbours.	6. Christians who go around evangelising can annoy people, so it does not help their cause.

2.11 Church growth

Essential information:

☐ Up to a third of the world's population claim to be Christian (including people who rarely attend church), and around 80,000 people become Christians each day.

☐ The Church expects new Christians to help spread the faith as part of their commitment to Jesus.

☐ Christ for all Nations is an example of a Christian organisation that promotes evangelism.

The growth of the Church

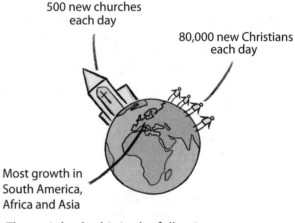

500 new churches each day

80,000 new Christians each day

Most growth in South America, Africa and Asia

- The Church is growing rapidly in South America, Africa and Asia, but not in the USA, Europe and the Middle East (where Christians have been persecuted).
- Worldwide around 80,000 people become Christians each day, and over 500 new churches are formed.
- The Church's mission is to make disciples, not just new believers. This means **new Christians are also expected to help spread the faith**.
- Evangelism should therefore be followed up by training new **converts** (people who decide to change their religious faith) in the way of following Jesus.
- Every Christian has a role in **encouraging fellow believers**. They might do this in the following ways.

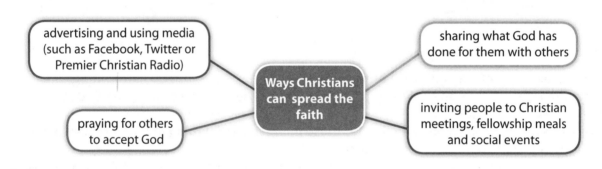

advertising and using media (such as Facebook, Twitter or Premier Christian Radio)

sharing what God has done for them with others

Ways Christians can spread the faith

praying for others to accept God

inviting people to Christian meetings, fellowship meals and social events

Christ for all Nations

- Christ for all Nations is an example of a **Christian organisation promoting evangelism**. They do this by holding evangelistic meetings throughout the world, but particularly in Africa.
- They are led by the evangelists Richard Bonnke and Daniel Kolenda.
- Some of their large open-air rallies held in Africa have drawn crowds of up to 1.6 million people.
- It is claimed that many miracles of healing take place at the meetings.
- Christ for all Nations claims that 74 million people have filled in decision cards to follow Christ at their meetings.

(A) Give **two** ways in which the Church gets its message to people.

(B) **Evaluate this argument** in response to the statement, 'Christians should just rely on evangelists for Church growth.' Explain your reasoning and suggest how you would improve the argument.

"Christians should not just rely on evangelists for Church growth because there are not that many specially trained evangelists to promote Christianity. People are more likely to be drawn to Christianity by the inspiration of someone they know, like a neighbour who is kind and considerate and demonstrates the love that Jesus taught."

TIP

You will not be asked a specific question about Christ for all Nations in your exam, but being able to give examples of the work of Christian organisations or charities may be very helpful.

Essential information:

☐ The worldwide Church has a mission to restore people's relationship with God and with one another.

☐ The Church therefore plays an important role in **reconciliation** (restoring harmony after relationships have broken down), through initiatives to develop peace and understanding.

Working for reconciliation

- Christians believe humans were **reconciled to God** through Jesus' death and resurrection. This means Jesus' death and resurrection helped to **restore the relationship between God and humanity**, which had been broken by sin (see page 22).
- For Catholics, the **sacrament of Reconciliation** also helps to restore people's relationship with God.
- Matthew 5:23–24 teaches that Christians should be **reconciled to each other**.
- Reconciliation is therefore an **important part of the Church's work**. This might involve anything from trying to restore relationships between individual people, to working for peace between different religious groups or nations at conflict.

> 66 For if, while we were God's enemies, we were reconciled to him through the death of his Son, how much more, having been reconciled, shall we be saved through his life! 99
>
> *Romans 5:10 [NIV]*

TIP

You could use this quote in your exam to show that humanity's relationship with God was restored (or reconciled) through the death of Jesus.

Examples of organisations working for reconciliation

- The **Irish Churches Peace Project** brings Catholics and Protestants together in Northern Ireland.
- The project aims to develop peace and understanding between these two denominations.

- The **World Council of Churches** works for reconciliation between different Christian denominations and members of other faiths.
- For example, the Pilgrimage of Justice and Peace initiative supports inter-religious dialogue and cooperation.

- After the bombing of Coventry Cathedral in World War II, local Christians showed forgiveness to those responsible, and the cathedral became a world centre for peace and reconciliation.
- The cathedral is home to the **Community of the Cross of Nails**, which works with partners in other countries to bring about peace and harmony.

- The **Corrymeela Community** brings together people from different backgrounds, including people of different faiths or political leanings.
- They meet at a residential centre in Northern Ireland to build trust and explore ways of moving away from violence so they can work together constructively.

APPLY

(A) Give **two** examples of how the Church has helped to work towards reconciliation.

(B) 'Reconciliation to God is more important than reconciliation to other people.'

Develop this argument to support the statement by explaining in more detail, adding an example, or referring to a relevant religious teaching or quotation.

"Reconciliation to God is more important because God is the Supreme Being. God will judge us when we die and if we are not sorry for our sins we will not receive eternal life with God in heaven."

2.13 Christian persecution

Essential information:

- [ ] Christians have faced **persecution** (hostility and ill-treatment) from the beginning of the Church, and Christians are still persecuted worldwide today.

- [ ] For some Christians, persecution can have positive effects: it can strengthen their faith, allow them to share in Jesus' sufferings, and even inspire others to become Christian.

- [ ] The Church helps those who are persecuted through prayer, practical help and financial support, and by raising awareness of persecution and campaigning against it.

What is persecution?

- The International Society for Human Rights estimates 80% of all acts of religious discrimination today are aimed at Christians.
- This persecution happens around the world, but particularly in countries such as North Korea, Somalia, Iraq and Syria.
- It might involve:
  - being forced to pay extra tax
  - job discrimination
  - being forbidden to build churches
  - attacks on Christian homes, churches and families, including murder.

> **TIP**
> These examples of the kinds of persecution Christians face will be helpful if you need to give an explanation of persecution in your exam.

Some Christian Responses to persecution

Response	Supporting quote from scripture
- For some Christians, persecution can have a **positive effect**, as it strengthens their faith and conviction. - It also allows them to share in the suffering of Jesus.	" I want to know Christ – yes, to know the power of his resurrection and participation in his sufferings " *(Philippians 3:10)* This quote shows that one way Christians can get to know Jesus is by sharing in his suffering.
- The Church believes it is important to **act against persecution**, by supporting persecuted Christians wherever possible and campaigning on their behalf.	" If one part suffers, every part suffers with it " *(1 Corinthians 12:26)* This quote refers to the Church. It shows that helping individual Christians also helps the whole Church.
- Christians are **encouraged to show love and forgiveness** towards their persecutors.	" Do not be overcome by evil, but overcome evil with good " *(Romans 12:21)* This quote shows that Christians should respond to evil with love.

Some ways the Church has helped persecuted Christians

- Christians have smuggled Bibles into the USSR (Russia) to strengthen and give comfort to persecuted Christians.
- The Barnabas Fund sends money to support people persecuted for their faith.
- Christian Solidarity Worldwide campaigns for religious freedom for all.

A Give **two** ways in which Christians support those in countries where it is forbidden to follow Jesus.

B **Develop** one religious argument and one non-religious argument in response to the statement, 'It is not possible to "rejoice and be glad" if you are suffering persecution.'

> **TIP**
> 'Develop' means you need to add some detail to your argument, for example by explaining it more fully and giving examples.

RECAP

Essential information:

☐ Christian charities follow the example and teaching of Jesus in working to relieve poverty.

☐ Christians believe they should show Jesus to the world through helping the disadvantaged.

☐ Three Christian charities that help the poor are Christian Aid, Tearfund and CAFOD.

Helping those in poverty

Christians try to help those living in poverty because Jesus taught that this was important. For example:

- Jesus once told a rich man to sell everything and give to the poor (Mark 10:21).
- The parable of the Rich Man and Lazarus tells of a rich man who ends up in hell for ignoring a beggar.
- The parable of the Good Samaritan teaches the importance of helping all people.
- Jesus helped outcasts such as lepers, tax collector and sinners.

> **❝** If anyone has material possessions and sees a brother or sister in need but has no pity on them, how can the love of God be in that person? Dear children, let us not love with words or speech but with actions and in truth. **❞**   *1 John 3:17–18 [NIV]*

TIP
You only need to know about one of these organisations for your exam.

Three Christian charities that help those in poverty are Christian Aid, Tearfund and CAFOD (Catholic Agency for Overseas Development). These charities:

Charity	Examples of their work
Christian Aid	• Supports projects to encourage sustainable development. • Provides emergency relief, such as food, water, shelter and sanitation. • Campaigns to end poverty alongside organisations such as the Fairtrade Foundation, Trade Justice and Stop Climate Chaos.
Tearfund	• Works with over 90,000 churches worldwide to help lift people out of poverty. • Supplies emergency aid after natural disasters and conflict. • Provides long-term aid to help communities become more self-reliant, such as education or new farming equipment. • Supported by donations, fundraising events and prayer from churches in the UK.
CAFOD	• Works with local organisations to train, supply and support communities to work their own way out of poverty. • Gives short-term aid such as food, water and shelter during conflicts and disasters. • Lobbies UK government and global organisations for decisions that respect the poorest. • Encourages Catholic schools and parishes to pray, give money and campaign for justice.

APPLY

A Here are two ways in which a worldwide Christian relief organisation carries out its mission overseas. **Develop one of the points** by adding more detail and by referring to a relevant religious teaching or quotation.

"One way that Christian Aid carries out its mission overseas is to provide emergency relief when there is a disaster."

"Another way they help is by setting up longer-term programmes that encourage sustainable development."

TIP
Emergency aid gives help such as food, water and temporary shelter to people immediately after a disaster. In contrast, long-term aid tries to help people to become more self-sufficient over a longer period of time.

B **Write a paragraph** either supporting or against the statement, 'Religious charities should just concentrate on emergency aid.' Include a Christian teaching in your answer.

Test the 1 mark question

1   Which **one** of the following is a type of worship that follows a set pattern?

A Informal worship   B Private worship

C Non-liturgical worship   D Liturgical worship   **[1 mark]**

2   Which **one** of the following is the festival that celebrates the incarnation of Jesus?

A Easter   B Good Friday   C Christmas   D Lent   **[1 mark]**

Test the 2 mark question

3   Give **two** ways in which the Church responds to world poverty.   **[2 marks]**

1) _____

2) _____

4   Give **two** reasons why prayer is important to Christians.   **[2 marks]**

1) _____

2) _____

Test the 4 mark question

5   Explain **two** contrasting ways in which Christians worship.   **[4 marks]**

● **Explain one way.**	Some Christians worship with other people in church on Sunday by going to a service called Holy Communion.
● Develop your explanation with more detail/an example/ reference to a religious teaching or quotation.	During the liturgy, they receive bread and wine that they believe is the body and blood of Jesus.
● **Explain a second contrasting way.**	Other Christians prefer informal worship, sometimes meeting in someone's home.
● Develop your explanation with more detail/an example/ reference to a religious teaching or quotation.	These Christians share their faith by reading and discussing a passage from scripture and praying together in their own words.

TIP
In this answer formal worship is contrasted with informal worship, but you could also contrast public worship with private worship or liturgical worship with charismatic worship.

6   Explain **two** contrasting ways in which Christians practise baptism.   **[4 marks]**

● **Explain one way.**	
● Develop your explanation with more detail/an example/ reference to a religious teaching or quotation.	
● **Explain a second contrasting way.**	
● Develop your explanation with more detail/an example/ reference to a religious teaching or quotation.	

TIP
The question asks for different 'ways' in which Christians practise baptism, not different beliefs about baptism. The clearest contrast is between believers' baptism and infant baptism, but you should focus your answer on the way each of these is carried out, not what people believe about them.

7   Explain **two** contrasting interpretations of the meaning of Holy Communion.   **[4 marks]**

2 Exam practice

Test the 5 mark question

8 Explain **two** ways that Christian charities help the poor in less economically developed countries.
Refer to sacred writings or another source of Christian belief and teaching in your answer.   **[5 marks]**

● **Explain one way.**	*One way that Christian charities help the poor in less economically developed countries is by providing emergency aid when there has been a natural disaster, like an earthquake or famine.*
● Develop your explanation with more detail/an example.	*For example, Tearfund, a Christian charity, was set up originally to provide emergency aid in response to the famine in Biafra, Nigeria, where it sent emergency food and clothing to refugees fleeing the famine-struck country.*
● **Explain a second way.**	*A second way that Christian charities help is by providing long-term aid that helps countries become self-sufficient or less dependent on aid.*
● Develop your explanation with more detail/an example.	*CAFOD, for example, works on development projects to give people access to education, healthcare, and clean water.*
● Add a reference to sacred writings or another source of Christian belief and teaching. If you prefer, you can add this reference to your first belief instead.	*These charities are inspired by Christian teachings such as the parable of the Rich Man and Lazarus, where Jesus taught that rich people who ignore the needs of the poor will be punished by God.*

TIP
Here the student has used a parable from the bible. Another 'source of Christian belief and teaching' could be official statements or documents by leaders of the Church.

9 Explain **two** reasons why Christians practise evangelism.
Refer to sacred writings or another source of Christian belief and teaching in your answer.   **[5 marks]**

● **Explain one reason.**	
● Develop your explanation with more detail/an example.	
● **Explain a second reason.**	
● Develop your explanation with more detail/an example.	
● Add a reference to sacred writings or another source of Christian belief and teaching. If you prefer, you can add this reference to your first teaching instead.	

TIP
It is helpful to start by explaining the meaning of 'evangelism' before explaining why Christians practise it.

10 Explain **two** ways that Christians may work for reconciliation.
Refer to sacred writings or another source of Christian belief and teaching in your answer.   **[5 marks]**

2 Exam practice

Test the 12 mark question

11 'The most important duty of the Church is to help people in need.'
Evaluate this statement. In your answer you should:
- refer to Christian teaching
- give reasoned arguments to support this statement
- give reasoned arguments to support a different point of view
- reach a justified conclusion.

[12 marks]

REASONED ARGUMENTS IN SUPPORT OF THE STATEMENT ● **Explain why some people would agree with the statement.** ● Develop your explanation with more detail and examples. ● Refer to religious teaching. Use a quote or paraphrase or refer to a religious authority. ● **Evaluate the arguments.** Is this a good argument or not? Explain why you think this.	*'The Church' in this statement clearly stands for the Christian believers and not the actual building. So what does the Bible say about the duty of Christians? Jesus taught his followers that helping those in need is extremely important and he showed he believed that by the way he acted. If he saw a person suffering from an illness he healed them. He touched lepers in order that they might be cured, even though it was something other people would not do because it was against the law and they feared catching leprosy. He gave sight to the blind, healed the crippled and even cast out evil spirits that were tormenting a naked madman. Jesus did this because he had compassion and pity on those he saw were in need.* *Jesus also showed in his teaching that Christians should help people in need. In the parable of the Good Samaritan it is the traveller who showed pity on the wounded man and helped him that is the hero of the story. Furthermore Jesus warns that those who do not help will face the anger of God on judgement day in the parable of the Sheep and the Goats. The sheep represented the people who helped and were given the reward of eternal life, but the goats did not and were thrown out of God's presence. So you could argue that it is the most important duty of the Church to help people who are in need.*
REASONED ARGUMENTS SUPPORTING A DIFFERENT VIEW ● **Explain why some people would support a different view.** ● Develop your explanation with more detail and examples. ● Refer to religious teaching. Use a quote or paraphrase or refer to a religious authority. ● **Evaluate the arguments.** Is this a good argument or not? Explain why you think this.	*On the other hand, Jesus summed up the duty for Christians and the Church in two commandments. He said that the first, most important commandment is to love God. The second is to love our neighbour as ourselves. If that is the case, then the most important duty of the Church (Christians) is to love and worship God, and this is more important than helping those in need.*
CONCLUSION ● **Give a justified conclusion.** ● Include your own opinion together with your own reasoning. ● **Include evaluation.** Explain why you think one viewpoint is stronger than the other or why they are equally strong. ● Do not just repeat arguments you have already used without explaining how they apply to your reasoned opinion/conclusion.	*In conclusion I would say that the statement is wrong and I would argue that the most important duty is to love God. The only way the Church can show love of God is by loving human beings who need help. So that is also important, but not the most important duty. It merely follows on from the most important duty.*

TIP
The student has develop[ed] this argument by referri[ng] to the Bible. Although th[ere] are no direct quotation[s] the answer shows excelle[nt] knowledge of Jesus' actio[ns] and teaching and uses these to support the statement.

TIP
This argument could be developed further for more marks. For example, it could go into more detail about other important duties of the Church (such as preaching the gospel or administering the sacraments), and explain why these are equally or more important than helping people in need.

12 'The best way for Christians to grow closer to God is to go on a pilgrimage.'

Evaluate this statement. In your answer you should:

- refer to Christian teaching
- give reasoned arguments to support this statement
- give reasoned arguments to support a different point of view
- reach a justified conclusion.

[12 marks]

> **TIP**
> Look for the key words in questions. Here it is 'best'. The answer should focus on whether or not a pilgrimage is the best way for Christians to grow closer to God or whether there are other ways that might be better.

REASONED ARGUMENTS IN SUPPORT OF THE STATEMENT ● **Explain why some people would agree with the statement.** ● Develop your explanation with more detail and examples. ● Refer to religious teaching. Use a quote or paraphrase or refer to a religious authority. ● **Evaluate the arguments.** Is this a good argument or not? Explain why you think this.	
REASONED ARGUMENTS SUPPORTING A DIFFERENT VIEW ● **Explain why some people would support a different view.** ● Develop your explanation with more detail and examples. ● Refer to religious teaching. Use a quote or paraphrase or refer to a religious authority. ● **Evaluate the arguments.** Is this a good argument or not? Explain why you think this.	
CONCLUSION ● **Give a justified conclusion.** ● Include your own opinion together with your own reasoning. ● **Include evaluation.** Explain why you think one viewpoint is stronger than the other or why they are equally strong. ● Do not just repeat arguments you have already used without explaining how they apply to your reasoned opinion/conclusion.	

13 'A Christian's most important duty is to tell others about their faith.'

Evaluate this statement. In your answer you should:

- refer to Christian teaching
- give reasoned arguments to support this statement
- give reasoned arguments to support a different point of view
- reach a justified conclusion.

[12 marks]

> **TIP**
> 'To tell others about their faith' is the meaning of evangelism, which is part of a Christian's mission. Try to use these terms in your answer to show the depth of your understanding about this topic.

Check your answers using the mark scheme on page 122. How did you do?

To feel more secure in the content you need to remember, re-read pages 28–41.

To remind yourself of what the examiner is looking for, go to pages 6–11.

3 Relationships and families

3.1 Christian teachings about human sexuality

RECAP

Essential information:

- [ ] **Human sexuality** refers to how people express themselves as sexual beings.
- [ ] **Heterosexual** relationships are between a man and a woman, members of the opposite sex.
- [ ] **Homosexual** relationships are between members of the same sex.

Contemporary British attitudes

- The age of consent (at which a person is legally old enough to freely agree to have sex) is 16 years old in Britain.
- Contraception and legal abortion have reduced fear or risk of pregnancy.
- Sex before marriage, multiple sex partners, children outside of marriage, affairs (adultery) or open homosexual relationships have become more common.
- Homosexual couples can legally marry.

> You might be asked to compare beliefs on homosexual relationships between Christianity (the main religious tradition in Great Britain) and another religious tradition.

Christian attitudes towards human sexuality

- The Christian Church teaches that marriage is the only valid place for heterosexual relationships because it is part of God's plan for humans (Genesis 1:28 and 2:24).
- Christian views about sex before marriage vary but all are against unfaithfulness.

> ❝ God blessed them and said to them, "Be fruitful and increase in number; fill the earth and subdue it." ❞
> *Genesis 1:28* [NIV]

> ❝ That is why a man leaves his father and mother and is united to his wife, and they become one flesh. ❞
> *Genesis 2:24* [NIV]

TIP
These quotations support reasons why many Christians are against sex before or outside of marriage.

- Christians who oppose homosexual relationships base their views on the Bible, where it is written that sex between two men is forbidden (Leviticus 18:22 and 1 Corinthian 6: 9–10).
- The Catholic Church teaches that homosexuals are not sinful, but should remain chaste (not have sex) to avoid sinful acts.
- The Church of England welcomes homosexuals living in committed relationships, but does not allow marriage in a church.
- Some Christians think the Bible needs to be interpreted in the context of modern society so think loving, faithful homosexual relationships are just as holy as heterosexual ones.
- The United Reformed Church allows its local churches, if they are in agreement, to perform marriages between homosexuals.

APPLY

A **Develop** the argument given below by explaining in more detail, adding an example, or referring to a relevant religious teaching or quotation.

"Some Christians believe that loving, faithful homosexual relationships are just as holy as heterosexual ones."

B **Develop this argument** to support the statement, 'Sex has been devalued in British society' by referring to one religious argument, and one non-religious argument.

"Nowadays many people in Britain have lots of sex partners or affairs. Sex is no longer seen as something special, a part of God's plan for human beings."

Essential information:

- **Sex before marriage** is sex between two single unmarried people.
- **Sex outside marriage** is sex between two people where one or both of them is married to someone else; **adultery** or having an affair.

Sexual relationships before marriage

- Sex before marriage is now widely accepted in British society, against the beliefs of many religious people.
- For many Christians, sex expresses a deep, lifelong union that requires the commitment of marriage and should not be a casual, temporary pleasure.
- Christians believe it is wrong to use people for sex, to spread sexually transmitted infections or to risk pregnancy.
- Anglican and Catholic churches teach that sex before marriage is wrong.
- Some liberal Christians, however, think that sex before marriage can be a valid expression of love for each other, particularly if the couple are intending marriage.

> Flee from sexual immorality. All other sins a person commits are outside the body, but whoever sins sexually, sins against their own body. Do you not know your bodies are temples of the Holy Spirit?
>
> *1 Corinthians 6:18–19 [NIV]*

You might be asked to compare beliefs on sexual relationships before marriage between Christianity (the main religious tradition in Great Britain) and another religious tradition.

TIP
You will need to make reference to Christianity and one other religious tradition, either from within Christianity or from another religion.

Sexual relationships outside marriage

- All religions teach that adultery is wrong as it involves lies and secrecy, and betrays trust.
- Adultery breaks the vows Christian couples make before God and threatens the stable relationship needed for their children's security.
- It is against one of the Ten Commandments and Jesus' teaching that lust, which could lead to adultery, is wrong.
- Jesus forgave a woman caught in adultery but ordered her to leave her life of sin.

> You shall not commit adultery.
>
> *Exodus 20:14 [NIV]*

> You have heard that it was said, "You shall not commit adultery." But I tell you that anyone who looks at a woman lustfully has already committed adultery with her in his heart.
>
> *Matthew 5:27–28 [NIV]*

> The sexual act must take place exclusively within marriage. Outside of marriage it always constitutes a grave sin.
>
> *Catechism 2390*

A Here are two religious beliefs about sexual relationships outside of marriage (adultery). **Develop** one of the points by referring to a relevant religious teaching or quotation.

"Christians think sex outside of marriage (adultery) is wrong because it breaks the vows couples make at their wedding."

"Christians also believe having an affair can affect children and cause pain to all concerned."

B **List two points** supporting and **two** points against the statement, 'It is not always wrong to have sex before marriage.' Develop one of them by adding more detail or an example.

3.3 Contraception and family planning

RECAP

Essential information:

☐ **Contraception** refers to the methods used to prevent a pregnancy taking place.

☐ **Family planning** is controlling how many children couples have and when they have them.

Contemporary British attitudes towards family planning

- There is widespread acceptance of artificial contraception to help family planning.
- Some believe in a personal responsibility to prevent unwanted pregnancies.
- There is concern for global overpopulation.
- Many religious people, e.g. Muslims and Jews also accept using some forms of contraception for certain reasons is acceptable.

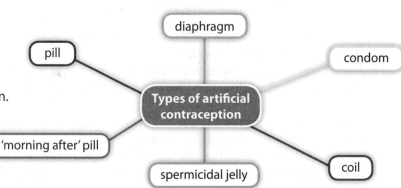

Christian attitudes towards family planning

Christian churches believe having children is God's greatest gift to married couples, but there are times when it may be acceptable to avoid bringing children into the world.

Religious group	Teaching	Methods
Catholic	• Artificial contraception goes against natural law/purpose of marriage • Could encourage selfishness/infidelity • Purposes of sex (having children and expressing love) should not be separated • Every sex act should be open to creating new life	• Rhythm method/ avoiding sex at fertile times of month
Orthodox	• Artificial contraception goes against natural law/purpose of marriage • Can encourage selfishness • Orthodox Church agrees with Catholic position but recognises individuals' needs	• Non-abortive forms of contraception only
Anglican and Non-conformist	• People should only have as many children as they can care for • Unfair to bring a baby into deprivation • Allow contraception to enable couples to develop relationship first/space out pregnancies to avoid harming mother's health • Anglican Lambeth Conference approved artificial contraception used 'in the light of Christian principles' (1930)	• Preference for non-abortive forms of contraception

> **"** Every sexual act should have the possibility of creating new life. **"**
> *Humanae Vitae*, 1968

You might be asked to compare beliefs on contraception between Christianity (the main religious tradition in Great Britain) and another religious tradition.

APPLY

A Give **two** religious beliefs about the use of contraception.

B **Evaluate this argument** against the statement, 'The Christian Church should not take a view on family planning.' Explain why this argument is weak. Suggest ways to improve it.

"The Christian Church has every right to have a view about family planning. Everyone is entitled to their own opinion. They can think what they like. They have the same rights as anyone else."

TIP
Simply write down two different beliefs. There is no need to go into detail.

RECAP

Essential information:

- **Marriage** is a legal union between a man and a woman (or in some countries, including the UK, two people of the same sex) as partners in a relationship.
- A **civil partnership** is a legal union of same-sex couples (2004).
- **Same-sex marriage** is marriage between partners of the same sex (2014).
- **Cohabitation** refers to a couple living together and having a sexual relationship without being married to one another.

Marriage

- Marriage, civil partnerships and same-sex marriage are legal contracts that protect each partner and provide legal and financial benefits.
- Many Christians oppose same-sex marriage because it redefines marriage to mean merely a committed relationship, rather than a unique bond between a man and woman that involves the creation of new life (children).
- Churches that oppose homosexual marriage are not forced by law to conduct them.
- In Britain many couples cohabit without getting married because:
  - the cost of marriage prevents people from marrying immediately
  - they want to see if the relationship will work
  - they don't believe in marriage as an institution.

The purpose of marriage for Christians

- The purpose of marriage is to provide a stable, secure environment for family life.
- Marriage is the proper place to enjoy sex, raise children in a religious faith and provide lifelong support and companionship for a partner.
- Catholic and Orthodox Churches oppose cohabitation as they believe sex should only take place within marriage.
- Many Anglican and Protestant Christians accept that although marriage is best, people may cohabit in a faithful, loving and committed way without being married.

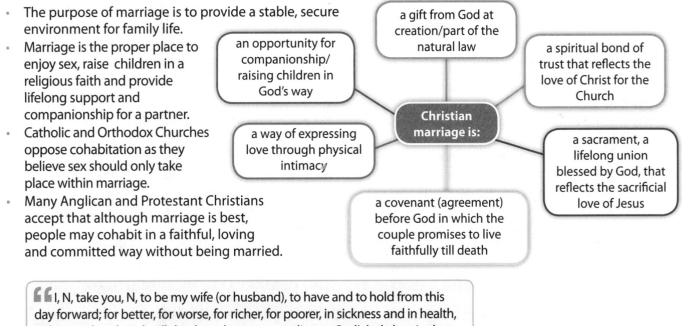

Christian marriage is:

- a gift from God at creation/part of the natural law
- a spiritual bond of trust that reflects the love of Christ for the Church
- an opportunity for companionship/raising children in God's way
- a way of expressing love through physical intimacy
- a sacrament, a lifelong union blessed by God, that reflects the sacrificial love of Jesus
- a covenant (agreement) before God in which the couple promises to live faithfully till death

> ❝ I, N, take you, N, to be my wife (or husband), to have and to hold from this day forward; for better, for worse, for richer, for poorer, in sickness and in health, to love and to cherish, till death us do part; according to God's holy law. In the presence of God I make this vow. ❞ *Anglican marriage service vows*

APPLY

A Here are two religious beliefs about the nature of marriage. **Develop one** of the beliefs by referring to a relevant religious teaching or quotation.

"Marriage is God's gift to human beings at creation."

"Marriage is the proper place to enjoy a sexual relationship."

B **Develop this argument** to support the statement, 'Marriage gives more stability to society than cohabitation' by explaining in more detail, adding an example or referring to a religious teaching.

"Marriage is a serious, lifelong public commitment that protects the rights of each partner and brings security to future children. Cohabitation does not protect the children or remaining parent if one partner decides to leave the relationship."

RECAP

Essential information:

☐ There are many reasons why a couple might **divorce** (legally end a marriage), for example, because of adultery, domestic abuse, illness, and so on.

☐ **Remarriage** is when someone marries again while their former husband or wife is still alive.

☐ Christians have to balance ethical arguments between the sanctity of marriage vows and compassion for people whose marriage is breaking down.

Reasons for divorce

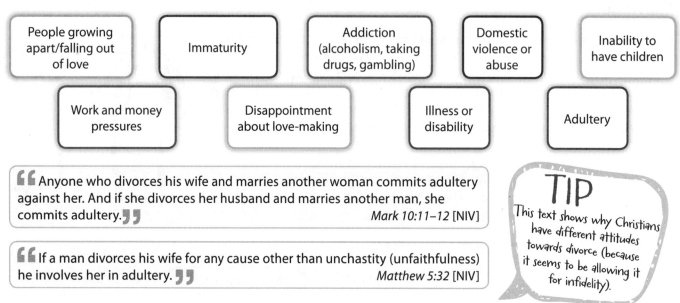

People growing apart/falling out of love

Immaturity

Addiction (alcoholism, taking drugs, gambling)

Domestic violence or abuse

Inability to have children

Work and money pressures

Disappointment about love-making

Illness or disability

Adultery

> " Anyone who divorces his wife and marries another woman commits adultery against her. And if she divorces her husband and marries another man, she commits adultery. "
> *Mark 10:11–12* [NIV]

> " If a man divorces his wife for any cause other than unchastity (unfaithfulness) he involves her in adultery. "
> *Matthew 5:32* [NIV]

TIP
This text shows why Christians have different attitudes towards divorce (because it seems to be allowing it for infidelity).

Christian teachings about divorce and remarriage

- Vows made in God's presence must be kept.
- The Catholic Church teaches that marriage is a sacrament between two baptised people that is permanent, lifelong and cannot be dissolved by civil divorce. Catholics can obtain an **annulment** if the church rules that the marriage was never valid.
- Other Christians believe marriage is for life, but sometimes divorce is the lesser of two evils.
- Divorced Anglicans can marry someone else in church with the bishop's permission and consent of the vicar.
- Other Protestant churches, e.g. Methodist or United Reformed Church, accept civil divorce and allow remarriage in church as long as the couple take the vows seriously. These Christians think the Church should reflect God's forgiveness and allow couples a second chance for happiness.
- The Eastern Orthodox Church grants divorce and remarries couples, but usually not more than twice.

Christian responses to couples who are having problems in their marriage

- Christian churches try to prevent marriage difficulties by offering courses that prepare couples for marriage.
- Clergy offer counselling, prayer and sacraments.
- Churches try to bring forgiveness and reconciliation back to marriages that have broken down.
- Clergy may refer couples to outside agencies such as Relate and Accord for advice and counselling.
- Fellow Christians try to support a couple through difficult times.

APPLY

(A) Here are two religious beliefs about divorce. **Develop one** of them by explaining in more detail and refer to a relevant religious teaching or quotation.

"Divorce is wrong because Christian couples make vows before God that should never be broken."

"Some Christians reluctantly accept divorce because it can be the lesser of two evils."

(B) 'Divorce is never right.' **Write a paragraph** to explain whether you agree or disagree with the statement.

RECAP

Essential information:

☐ There are many types of **families** (people related by blood, marriage or adoption):

- **nuclear family** (a couple and their children)
- **stepfamily** (formed on the remarriage of a divorced or widowed person that includes a child/children)
- **extended family** (includes grandparents or other relatives beyond just parents and children).

☐ Parents have a vital role in bringing up their children physically, emotionally, morally and spiritually.

The role of parents

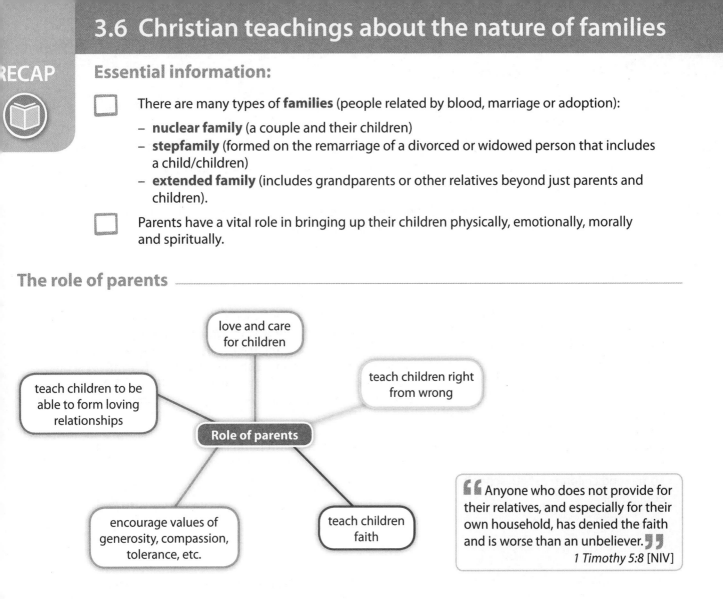

love and care for children

teach children to be able to form loving relationships

teach children right from wrong

Role of parents

encourage values of generosity, compassion, tolerance, etc.

teach children faith

> 66 Anyone who does not provide for their relatives, and especially for their own household, has denied the faith and is worse than an unbeliever. 99
> *1 Timothy 5:8* [NIV]

Christian teachings about the nature of families

- Christians must 'love one another'; it is in the family that a child learns to love.
- In Biblical times, people lived in extended families through which the religion, customs and traditions were passed to the next generation. All generations contributed to the welfare of the extended family.
- The Commandment 'Honour your father and mother' (Exodus 20:12) is important, particularly when parents are elderly and need support.
- There are examples of **polygamy** (the custom of having more than one wife at the same time) in the Bible, but Christians believe one man and one woman for life was created at the beginning.
- Polygamous marriages cannot be performed in Britain as **bigamy** (marrying someone while already married to another person) is illegal.
- Some traditional Christians disapprove of **same-sex parents** (people of the same sex who are raising children together); they believe that the ideal is for children to grow up with a male and female role model as parents.
- Other Christians think it is more important for children to be in a secure and loving family regardless of the gender of their parents.

APPLY

A Give **two** religious beliefs about the nature of the family.

B Develop **two** religious arguments that could be made to support the statement 'The most important thing when raising children is love.'

TIP
In this question, 'the nature of the family' means what the family should ideally be like.

RECAP

Essential information:

- [ ] The family is the main building block of society where **procreation** (bringing babies into the world) takes place.

- [ ] Happy, healthy families create **stability** (safety and security) for their members and society.

- [ ] An important purpose of the family is the **protection of children** (keeping children safe from harm).

- [ ] For Christians, a purpose of the family is **educating children in their faith** – bringing up children according to the religious beliefs of the parents.

The purpose of families

- The family is where people learn to live as part of a community, teach children right and wrong and how to get along with others.
- Christians believe God reveals himself as Father, with Jesus his Son and humankind his children, so the idea of the family is very important.
- Christian parents are expected to be good role models, teach children their faith, pray with them, teach them moral values and nurture their spiritual lives.
- Some send children to faith schools or groups run by their church for religious education.

> ❝ The family remains the most important grouping human beings have ever developed. **Children thrive, grow and develop within the love and safeguarding of a family.** Within the family we care for the young, the old and those with caring needs. **Families** should be able to **offer** each of their members **commitment, fun, love, companionship and security.** ❞
>
> *Church of England website*

TIP
This quote would support an answer on the purpose of families.

Relationships in Christian families

- The family reflects Christ's relationship with the Church.
- Parents and children have responsibilities to each other.
- Children are gifts from God so parents must respect their dignity.
- Children have duties to obey, love and respect their parents for their care.

> ❝ Husbands, love your wives, just as Christ loved the Church and gave himself up for her. ❞
>
> *Ephesians 5:25* [NIV]

> ❝ Children, obey your parents in everything, for this pleases the Lord. Fathers, do not embitter your children, or they will become discouraged. ❞
>
> *Colossians 3:20–21* [NIV]

> ❝ Listen to your father, who gave you life, and do not despise your mother when she is old. ❞
>
> *Proverbs 23:22* [NIV]

APPLY

A Here are two religious beliefs about the role of parents in a religious family. **Develop both points** by explaining in more detail, adding an example, and referring to a relevant quotation from scripture or sacred writings.

"Christian parents teach their children moral values."

"Christian parents bring up their children in their faith."

B **Evaluate this argument** to support the statement 'Families do not do enough for their elderly relatives in Britain today.'

"When children leave home, go to college and perhaps move away from their parents, they may not realise the difficulties this can cause when their parents become old and infirm. If they live far away, they may not be able to do very much for their elderly relatives. Christians, though, believe that they must 'Honour their father and mother' so they should still try to support elderly family members financially, take the time to Skype so that they feel part of the family, even if living far away, and keep their parents in their prayers."

3.8 Christian beliefs about gender equality

Essential information:

- **Gender equality** means that men and women should be given the same rights and opportunities as each other.

- Some things stand in its way:
  - **gender prejudice** (unfairly judging someone before the facts are known; holding biased opinions about people based on their gender)
  - **sexual stereotyping** (having a fixed idea of how men and women will behave)
  - **gender discrimination** (acting against someone on the basis of their gender; usually seen as wrong and may be against the law).

- Christians believe God created everyone as equals in the image of God.

The roles of men and women

- In the past, men held power and had more rights than women.
- Traditional roles saw men working to support the family, while women cared for the home and raised any children.
- The Sex Discrimination Act (1975) made gender discrimination illegal.
- Roles are changing as more women work, and housework and childcare are shared.

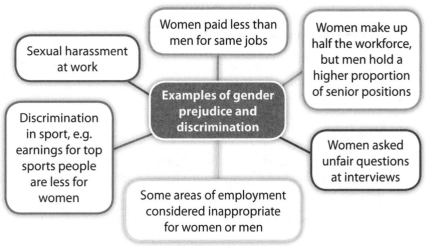

Christian beliefs and responses

- All people are created equal in the image of God.
- The command to love one's neighbour shows that discrimination is wrong.
- Jesus treated women with respect, welcomed them as disciples and showed, in the story of Martha and Mary, that they were capable of more than domestic tasks (Luke 10:38–42).
- Paul taught that all people are equal in Galatians 3:28.
- Some traditional Christians interpret Bible texts literally and think husbands should rule over their wives (Genesis 3:16).
- Most Christians today see marriage as an equal partnership.

> ❝There is neither Jew nor Gentile, neither slave nor free, nor is there male and female, for you are all one in Christ Jesus.❞
> *Galatians 3:28* [NIV]

> ❝So God created mankind in his own image, in the image of God he created them; male and female he created them.❞
> *Genesis 1:27* [NIV]

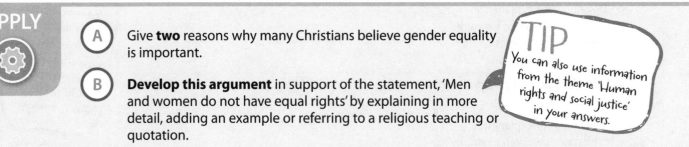

A Give **two** reasons why many Christians believe gender equality is important.

B **Develop this argument** in support of the statement, 'Men and women do not have equal rights' by explaining in more detail, adding an example or referring to a religious teaching or quotation.

TIP You can also use information from the theme 'Human rights and social justice' in your answers.

"Despite the Sex Discrimination Act making gender discrimination illegal, women still get paid less than men for similar jobs. Often women face unfair questions at interviews. Looking at big businesses, there are still many more men than women in top positions. Even some religions expect women to stay at home and look after children which prevents them from pursuing a career."

Test the 1 mark question

1 Which **one** of the following is **not** a reason why some marriages fail?

   A domestic violence   B adultery   C addiction   D stability   **[1 mark]**

2 Which **one** of the following describes a nuclear family?

   A a couple, children and grandparents   B a couple and their children

   C a couple, children, aunts and uncles   D a couple without children   **[1 mark]**

Test the 2 mark question

3 Give **two** religious beliefs about gender equality.   **[2 marks]**

   1) _____

   2) _____

4 Give **two** religious beliefs about cohabitation.   **[2 marks]**

   1) _____

   2) _____

> **TIP**
> Remember the main religious tradition of Great Britain is Christianity.

Test the 4 mark question

5 Explain **two** contrasting beliefs in contemporary British society about sex before marriage. In your answer you should refer to the main religious tradition of Great Britain and one or more other religious traditions.   **[4 marks]**

● **Explain one belief.**	*Some Christians believe that sex before marriage is all right if the couple has a committed, loving relationship.*
● Develop your explanation with more detail/an example/ reference to a religious teaching or quotation.	*Although they think it is better to get married, they accept that people can be faithful to each other and committed to the relationship even if they have not been officially married.*
● **Explain a second contrasting belief.**	*Muslims do not agree with sex before marriage because their holy book, the Qur'an, expressly forbids it.*
● Develop your explanation with more detail/an example/ reference to a religious teaching or quotation.	*They think that children have a right to be born into a secure family and that sex before marriage can lower the dignity of the people involved.*

> **TIP**
> It is important to say 'some' here, as many Christians, including the Orthodox and Catholic Churches, disapprove of sex before marriage.

6 Explain **two** contrasting religious beliefs about divorce. In your answer you must refer to one or more religious traditions.   **[4 marks]**

● **Explain one belief.**	
● Develop your explanation with more detail/an example/ reference to a religious teaching or quotation.	
● **Explain a second contrasting belief.**	
● Develop your explanation with more detail/an example/ reference to a religious teaching or quotation.	

> **TIP**
> You can answer this question from the perspective of two denominations of Christianity or from two religions.

7 Explain **two** contrasting religious beliefs about human sexuality.

In your answer you must refer to one or more religious traditions.   **[4 marks]**

3 Exam practice

Test the 5 mark question

8 Explain **two** religious beliefs about the nature of marriage.

Refer to sacred writings or another source of religious belief and teaching in your answer. **[5 marks]**

● **Explain one belief.**	*Christians believe that marriage is a unique relationship between a man and a woman that involves their ability to create new life in the form of children.*
● Develop your explanation with more detail/an example.	*They believe that God planned marriage from the beginning of creation when he told the first parents to be fruitful and increase in number, meaning to have children.*
● **Explain a second belief.**	*A second Christian belief about the nature of marriage is that marriage is a sacrament.*
● Develop your explanation with more detail/an example.	*This means that marriage is a lifelong union blessed by God, because the couple makes promises before God that they will be faithful to each other 'till death us do part'.*
● Add a reference to sacred writings or another source of religious belief and teaching. If you prefer, you can add this reference to your first belief instead.	*The Bible reflects this idea when it says, 'That is why a man leaves his father and mother and is united to his wife, and they become one flesh.' (Genesis 2:24)*

> **TIP**
> This quotation is from Genesis 2:24. There is no need to put the exact reference in your answer as long as you quote or paraphrase the passage.

9 Explain **two** religious beliefs about the purpose of families.

Refer to sacred writings or another source of religious belief and teaching in your answer. **[5 marks]**

● **Explain one belief.**	
● Develop your explanation with more detail/an example.	
● **Explain a second belief.**	
● Develop your explanation with more detail/an example.	
● Add a reference to sacred writings or another source of religious belief and teaching. If you prefer, you can add this reference to your first belief instead.	

10 Explain **two** religious beliefs about the role of children in a religious family.

Refer to sacred writings or another source of religious belief and teaching in your answer. **[5 marks]**

Test the 12 mark question

11 'The love and care parents show in bringing up their children is all that matters; the sex of the parents is unimportant.'

Evaluate this statement. In your answer you:

- should give reasoned arguments in support of this statement
- should give reasoned arguments to support a different point of view
- should refer to religious arguments
- may refer to non-religious arguments
- should reach a justified conclusion.

[12 marks]

Plus SPaG 3 ma

REASONED ARGUMENTS SUPPORTING A DIFFERENT VIEW	It is true that the love and care parents show in bringing up their children is the most important thing for a good family life. Without love and care, children would grow up deprived of stability and security. But the statement says 'the sex of the parents is unimportant' and that is where people may have different views.
● **Explain why some people would support a different view.**	
● Develop your explanation with more detail and examples.	Some Christians and Jews disapprove of same-sex parents because they think God made people male and female so that they would 'be fruitful and increase in number' (Genesis 1:28). Same-sex couples cannot do this naturally. Some also think the ideal for children is to grow up with a male and female role model as parents. Muslims believe that homosexual relationships are morally wrong so do not approve of such couples raising children. An important role of religious parents is to bring up their children in their faith. If their religion disagrees with homosexual relationships, then it is difficult for same-sex parents to bring their children up within the religion that disapproves of their behaviour.
● Refer to religious teaching. Use a quote or paraphrase or refer to a religious authority.	
● **Evaluate the arguments.** Is this a good argument or not? Explain why you think this.	
REASONED ARGUMENTS IN SUPPORT OF THE STATEMENT	On the other hand, many liberal Christians and Reform Jews think that it is more important that children are raised in a secure and loving family regardless of the gender of their parents. There is nothing to say same-sex parents are not religious even if particular faiths disapprove of their relationships. Many can still bring their children up to love God or live spiritual and morally good lives.
● **Explain why some people would agree with the statement.**	
● Develop your explanation with more detail and examples.	
● Refer to religious teaching. Use a quote or paraphrase or refer to a religious authority.	
● **Evaluate the arguments.** Is this a good argument or not? Explain why you think this.	
CONCLUSION	In conclusion, I think that whether parents are good at bringing up children depends on the individuals and not on their gender. Some heterosexual couples spoil their children or even abuse them which does not show good parenting. Many children live in single-parent families so do not have the benefit of a male and female role model anyway. The most important thing any family should have is love, and this is at the heart of all religions.
● **Give a justified conclusion.**	
● Include your own opinion together with your own reasoning.	
● **Include evaluation.** Explain why you think one viewpoint is stronger than the other or why they are equally strong.	
● Do not just repeat arguments you have already used without explaining how they apply to your reasoned opinion/conclusion.	

TIP
The question says you should 'refer to religious arguments' in your answe Your answer can refer t Christianity only, or it ca include references to othe religions.

TIP
Religious attitudes to some issues vary withi religions as well as betw religions, so it helps to 'some Christians' or 'lib Christians' to show y understand that not Christians share the sa views.

12 'Marriage is the proper place to enjoy a sexual relationship.'

Evaluate this statement. In your answer you:

- should give reasoned arguments in support of this statement
- should give reasoned arguments to support a different point of view
- should refer to religious arguments
- may refer to non-religious arguments
- should reach a justified conclusion.

[12 marks]
Plus SPaG 3 marks

REASONED ARGUMENTS IN SUPPORT OF THE STATEMENT

- **Explain why some people would agree with the statement.**

- Develop your explanation with more detail and examples.

- Refer to religious teaching. Use a quote or paraphrase or refer to a religious authority.

- **Evaluate the arguments.** Is this a good argument or not? Explain why you think this.

REASONED ARGUMENTS SUPPORTING A DIFFERENT VIEW

- **Explain why some people would support a different view.**

- Develop your explanation with more detail and examples.

- Refer to religious teaching. Use a quote or paraphrase or refer to a religious authority.

- **Evaluate the arguments.** Is this a good argument or not? Explain why you think this.

CONCLUSION

- **Give a justified conclusion.**

- Include your own opinion together with your own reasoning.

- **Include evaluation.** Explain why you think one viewpoint is stronger than the other or why they are equally strong.

- Do not just repeat arguments you have already used without explaining how they apply to your reasoned opinion/conclusion.

> **TIP**
> When evaluating a statement like this one, do not simply list what different people think about the issue, for example 'Christians would agree that the best place to enjoy sex is in marriage. Muslims also think ...' Remember to explain the reasons why they hold these opinions and to add an evaluation of how convincing you find these views to be.

13 'It is wrong for religious couples to use artificial contraception within marriage.'

Evaluate this statement. In your answer you:

- should give reasoned arguments in support of this statement
- should give reasoned arguments to support a different point of view
- should refer to religious arguments
- may refer to non-religious arguments
- should reach a justified conclusion.

[12 marks]
Plus SPaG 3 marks

Check your answers using the mark scheme on page 123. How did you do?

To feel more secure in the content you need to remember, re-read pages 46–53.

To remind yourself of what the examiner is looking for, go to pages 6–11.

4.1 Origins and value of the universe and the world

RECAP

Essential information:

☐ The story in Genesis 1.1–2.3 describes the creation of the universe.

☐ Scientists have put forward the Big Bang theory to explain how the universe began.

☐ Christians believe the earth to be valuable because God created it.

☐ Many Christians believe in the Big Bang theory and also that God created the universe.

The creation of the universe

Christians believe the **universe**, including all the planets, galaxies and everything in them, was designed and made by God out of nothing. The creation story in Genesis says that God created the world in six days and rested on the seventh.

- **Fundamentalist Christians** believe that the statements in the Bible are literally true. Some believe the creation stories describe exactly how the universe was created. Others believe that the seven days describe seven long periods of time.
- **Liberal Christians** believe that the Bible's authors were guided by God, but that not everything they wrote is a literal account of what actually happened. They believe that the creation stories are symbolic, where the main message is that God created the universe. They might look to science to understand *how* God did this.

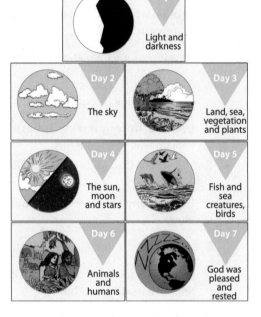

The Big Bang theory

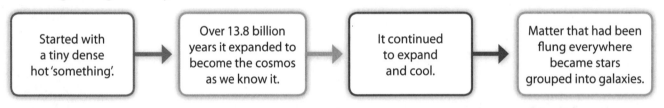

| Started with a tiny dense hot 'something'. | Over 13.8 billion years it expanded to become the cosmos as we know it. | It continued to expand and cool. | Matter that had been flung everywhere became stars grouped into galaxies. |

Both the creation story and Big Bang theory leave many questions unanswered and neither can be proved.

How valuable is the world?

For Christians, the earth is a priceless gift from God. The beauty of the world can give a sense of **awe** and **wonder**; devout respect for God's power of creation and marvelling at the complexity of the universe.

> "When I consider your heavens… what is mankind that you are mindful of them, human beings that you care for them?"
> *Psalm 8:3–4 [NIV]*

APPLY

A Here are two contrasting beliefs about how the world was created. **Develop each point:**

1) Fundamentalist Christians believe that the creation stories in the Bible describe exactly how the world was created.

2) Liberal Christians do not believe the Bible stories describe exactly how the world was created.

B 'It is not possible to believe both in the Genesis story of creation and in the Big Bang theory'.

Evaluate this statement, giving at least **two** arguments for two different points of view.

TIP
You do not need to accept the theories to be able to write about them in your exam.

4.2 Stewardship, dominion and the use of the environment

Essential information:

☐ Christians believe that people have a duty to protect and care for the earth and its environment; this is known as **stewardship**.

☐ Christians believe that God has given power and authority to humans to manage the earth; this is known as **dominion**.

☐ Abuse of natural resources is a problem today.

Stewardship

- Stewardship means that believers have a duty to look after the environment on behalf of God. Genesis 2 describes how Adam, the first man on earth, was given the role of stewardship over the earth, looking after it for God.

> ❝ The Lord God took the man (Adam) and put him in the Garden of Eden to work it and take care of it. ❞
> *Genesis 2:15 [NIV]*

- This responsibility has been passed down to mankind which means it is the role of all humans to look after the earth for God. If they use it wrongly, they are destroying what belongs to God.
- In return for looking after the earth, humans are allowed to use it to sustain life.

Dominion

- Christians teach that God gave humans power and authority to rule the world. This is called dominion.

> ❝ Rule over the fish in the sea and the birds in the sky and over every living creature that moves on the ground. ❞
> *Genesis 1:28 [NIV]*

- A minority interpret this as meaning that humans can do whatever they want because they are in charge.
- Most people are more interested in looking after the earth as stewards of God's earth.

Use of natural resources

- Genesis 1:31 shows that God values the earth he made.
- However, forests are being destroyed (**deforestation**). Natural **non-renewable resources** such as oil, coal and gas are being used up and will eventually run out.

> ❝ God saw all that he had made, and it was very good. ❞
> *Genesis 1: 31 [NIV]*

- As the world's population increases it's important to encourage **sustainable development**, progress that tries to reduce the impact on the natural world for future generations. Scientists are developing **renewable energies** from sources that won't run out, such as wind or solar energy.

Reduce, reuse, recycle

Christians believe they should avoid waste, conserve energy and reduce the demand for natural resources. Some examples of how this can be done are:

- turning off unused electrical appliances
- walking or cycling instead of driving
- reusing bags when shopping
- recycling waste, e.g. glass and paper.

APPLY

(A) What does stewardship mean?

(B) 'The idea of stewardship is more likely to encourage people to look after the earth than the idea of dominion.'

Give **two** reasons to agree with this and develop each one.

TIP
'Stewardship' and 'dominion' have specific religious meanings in the context of Christianity. The examiner will be impressed if you can use these terms accurately.

RECAP

Essential information:

- [ ] Air, land and water pollution are a major threat to life on earth.
- [ ] Many Christians show their concern by taking action to help to protect the earth.
- [ ] Religious leaders have met at Assisi and Ohito to discuss how to protect the earth.

What are the main types of pollution?

Pollution means contamination of something, especially the environment. As the use of technology increases and the world's population grows, pollution becomes more of a problem, putting human and animal life at risk.

Pollution type	Cause	Possible problems caused
Air	Fumes from factories and transport	Global warming, climate change, acid rain, diseases such as asthma and lung cancer.
Land	Poor disposal of waste	Chemicals pollute the earth causing wildlife to be poisoned, inefficient farming and poisoned food.
Water	Dumping waste into rivers and seas	Oil spills and plastic waste kill birds and marine life including whales.

What do Christians believe?

- The world is on loan to humans, who have been given the responsibility by God to look after it (Genesis 1:28).
- The parable of the Talents/Bag of Gold (Matthew 25:14–30) warns that God will be the final judge about how responsible humans have been in looking after the earth.
- Pollution is not loving towards others – 'Love your neighbour' (Luke 10:27 [NIV]).

> **❝** The earth is the Lord's and everything in it. **❞**
> *Psalm 24:1* [NIV]

TIP
If writing about what Christians believe, it is good to include and explain a quote or paraphrase rather than just providing a vague idea.

What do Christians do about the environment?

- Pope Francis wrote 'On the Care of Our Common Home', challenging people to tackle pollution, climate change and poverty. He stressed the need to reduce pollution, use renewable energy and recycle.
- In **1986**, religious leaders **met at Assisi** in Italy to discuss how religious people everywhere could help to care for the environment.
- As part of their statement in the Assisi Declarations on Nature, Christians wrote: 'Every human act of irresponsibility towards creatures is an abomination [disgrace]' (Alliance of Religions and Conservation).
- They **met again in Ohito** in Japan in **1995** where they stressed that being in charge of creation does not give people the right to abuse, spoil, waste or destroy the earth.
- Christian groups **work in and with their communities** to clean up the local environment, and may join secular environmental organisations such as Greenpeace and Friends of the Earth.

APPLY

A Explain **two** Christian beliefs about why polluting the earth is wrong.

Refer to sacred writings or another source of religious belief and teaching in your answer.

B 'Christians should not worry about pollution.' **Improve this argument** against the statement by developing the points made, including making the Bible teaching relevant:

"Christians should do a lot to solve pollution because the parable of the Talents warns that God will be the final judge about how responsible people have been in looking after the earth. They can use their talents to reduce pollution by changing how they live their lives."

Essential information:

☐ Christians believe animals were created by God for humans to use and care for.

☐ Christian hold different viewpoints about issues such as animal experimentation and using animals for food.

Animal experimentation

Many Christians are concerned about how animals are treated and whether it is necessary to harm or kill them. Genesis 9:3 gives permission for humans to eat meat, but Proverbs 12:10 says that humans should care for animals. The Bible's teachings can be interpreted in different ways.

- Scientists use animals such as rats, mice, chimpanzees and rabbits to test new products such as medicines and food, to make sure they are safe for humans to use.
- These animals are usually bred especially for the purpose of testing.
- Most Christians believe that if testing is proved to be necessary and provided the welfare of the animals is considered, it is justified to ensure human safety. Some believe that human life is sacred and using animals to develop new drugs may save many lives.
- However, alternative methods using computers and cell culture using artificially grown cells are being developed and fewer animals are being tested on.

Hindus believe all living creatures have souls so they must be protected and not experimented upon.

> You might be asked to compare beliefs on animal experimentation between Christianity (the main religious tradition in Great Britain) and another religious tradition.

> **TIP**
> You will need to make reference to Christianity and one other religious tradition, either from within Christianity or from another religion.

Should Christians eat meat?

- Christianity has no rules about whether Christians can eat meat or not.
- Many Christians believe that God gave humans animals for food and are happy to eat meat. However, they also believe that all views about diet should be respected.

> " The one who eats everything (including meat) must not treat with contempt the one who does not, and the one who does not eat everything must not judge the one who does, for God has accepted them. "
> *Romans 14:3* [NIV]

- Those that don't eat meat or fish are called **vegetarians**. Many vegetarians believe that it is wrong to kill animals for food or to be cruel to animals, for example through factory farming.
- Some people (**vegans**) will not eat or use anything from an animal including milk, eggs and leather. Many believe it is wrong to use animals in any way, including using products that may have brought harm to animals.
- Non-meat eaters, including some Christians, say there is no need to eat animals because a non-meat diet provides all the nutrition humans need.
- Some point out that if crops were grown on land currently used to raise animals for meat, there would be much more food to go round and this would please God.

(A) Explain **two** reasons why some Christians do not eat meat.

(B) 'Christians believe that experimenting on animals is wrong because it is cruel.'

Put forward an argument in favour of the statement and **develop** it with Christian teachings, explaining how the teachings are relevant to the argument.

> **TIP**
> In a 12 mark answer, always show how the religious teaching is relevant to the point you are making.

RECAP

Essential information:

☐ Religion and science both attempt to explain the origins of human life.

☐ Many Christians believe it is possible to believe both the creation story and the theory of evolution.

Adam and Eve

- Genesis 1 says that God created all life with human life being created last.
- Genesis 2 describes how God created the first man, Adam, from the soil and breathed life into him.
- Adam was given responsibility to look after his environment – the Garden of Eden.
- Some time later, while Adam was asleep, God took one of his ribs and used it to create a woman, Eve. God intended Eve to help Adam, and that they would live in a close relationship with each other and with him.

Some Christians do not believe the creation accounts in Genesis to be literally true (although others believe that they are), and many interpret it as showing that humans are very special to God because they were created in his image. They have a spiritual nature just as God does and unlike any other living creatures can relate to God in a special way.

What does science say?

In 1859, in a book called *The Origin of Species by Means of Natural Selection,* Charles Darwin put forward the theory of evolution. Darwin suggested that as the earth cooled, conditions became right to support life. The diagram shows the process.

| Life started with single-celled creatures in the sea. | → | Over a long period of time they evolved (changed) into creatures capable of living on land. | → | Next came creatures with the ability to fly, such as insects and birds. | → | Around 2.5 million years ago creatures resembling humans formed. | → | They gradually changed into humans about 200,000 years ago. |

Creatures were able to change or **adapt** to their environment and bred successfully, passing on their favourable genes to their offspring. This is called the 'survival of the fittest'.

What do Christians believe?

Fundamentalist Christians believe God created each species separately.

> Some do not believe in the 'survival of the fittest' or that different species evolved from each other. They question why some adapted better than others to their environment and they think there is insufficient evidence for evolution.

The majority of Christians accept both the Bible story of creation and Darwin's theory of evolution.

> They believe God is the creator who started the process. The theory of evolution explains how the beginnings of life set in motion by God have developed over millions of years and will continue to change for as long as the earth exists.

APPLY

A Explain **two** teachings gained from the Bible story of creation and two from scientific theory.

B Choose one of the above theories, or a combination of both of them, and give your opinion on whether you agree with it. **Write two developed reasons** to support your opinion.

TIP

Remember that Genesis 1 and 2 and the theory of evolution are trying to answer slightly different questions, a point you can use in an evaluation.

RECAP

Essential information:

☐ **Abortion** – removing a foetus from the womb to end a pregnancy – is legal in the UK if doctors agree that it meets certain criteria.

The legal position

- In 1990, the Human Fertilisation and Embryology Act set various conditions to govern abortion.
- An abortion must take place in a licensed clinic and only during the first 24 weeks of the pregnancy.
- The 24-week limit does not apply if the mother's life is in danger or if the foetus is severely deformed.
- Two doctors must agree to it taking place but only if it meets at least one of the following conditions:

1. Pregnancy endangers the woman's life.	2. The woman's physical or mental health is endangered.	3. There is a strong risk that the baby will be born with severe physical or mental disabilities.	4. An additional child may endanger the physical or mental health of other children in the family.

What do Christians believe?

- Christians believe in the **sanctity of life**, that all life is holy. This means they believe that, as humans are made in the image of God, their life is sacred, precious and a God-given blessing.
- The quote from Jeremiah 1:5 can be interpreted as meaning that God gives people a purpose in life. Abortion takes this away.
- The Catholic Church, along with many evangelical Christians, believes that abortion is wrong because life begins at conception so abortion is taking away life.
- Other Christians believe it is the lesser of two evils. If abortion is the kindest option, for example in instances of rape or if the baby will have a very poor quality of life, they may support it.

> " Before I formed you in the womb I knew you, before you were born I set you apart. "
> *Jeremiah 1:5* [NIV]

You might be asked to compare beliefs on abortion between Christianity (the main religious tradition in Great Britain) and another religious tradition.

Arguments for and against abortion

For	Against
• Pro-choice groups believe that the woman's life is more important. The woman has to carry the baby, give birth to it and bring it up, so she should have the right to choose whether to give birth to it. • Life doesn't start until birth (or viability – around 26 weeks) so abortion does not involve killing. • It is cruel to allow a severely disabled child to live.	• Pro-life groups argue that life begins at conception. All DNA required to create a unique individual is present at conception. Therefore abortion is killing life. • Disabled children can enjoy a good **quality of life** and have good general well-being. • The unborn child needs to be protected. • Unwanted children can be adopted. • Those who choose abortion can suffer from depression and guilt afterwards.

APPLY

A Explain **two** legal points that are used to decide whether an abortion should be allowed.

B 'If the quality of life is not going to be good, abortion is the best option.'

Write and fully develop an argument to support each of two different points of view about this quote.

TIP
The commandment 'you shall not kill' is often used when discussing abortion. If you use it, explain that it is only relevant if life begins at conception or some point before an abortion happens.

4.7 Euthanasia

Essential information:

☐ **Euthanasia** means 'a good or gentle death', painlessly ending the life of someone who is dying.

☐ Many Christians believe that taking a life is wrong but some believe that euthanasia may be acceptable in certain circumstances.

What is euthanasia?

Active euthanasia involves taking deliberate steps to end a person's life, for example by giving a lethal injection. This is illegal in the UK. There are three main types of euthanasia:

> You might be asked to compare beliefs on euthanasia between Christianity (the main religious tradition in Great Britain) and another religious tradition.

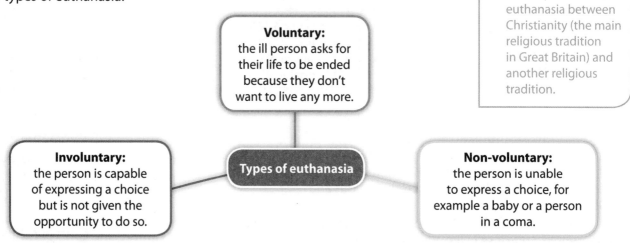

Voluntary: the ill person asks for their life to be ended because they don't want to live any more.

Involuntary: the person is capable of expressing a choice but is not given the opportunity to do so.

Types of euthanasia

Non-voluntary: the person is unable to express a choice, for example a baby or a person in a coma.

- Doctors can decide to withhold treatment if it is in the patient's best interests, for example by not resuscitating a person after a heart attack or withdrawing food. This would not be considered euthanasia as it is allowing death to take place, rather than actively ending a life.

Christian beliefs

Some Christians believe that euthanasia may be acceptable in some cases to end a person's suffering, but many believe it is never right to take a life.

Arguments in favour	Arguments against
• Drugs to end life are God-given so can be used.	• Euthanasia is deliberate killing, murder, and interferes with God's plan.
• God gives people free will to end their own life.	• It is open to abuse and may be against the will of the ill person.
• Euthanasia may be the most loving and compassionate thing to do, following Jesus' teaching: 'Love your neighbour.' (Luke 10:27 [NIV])	• It disrespects the sanctity of life. • Only God should take life, at the time of his choosing.
• Euthanasia allows a good and gentle death which may not be the case if natural death occurs.	• It breaks God's commandment: 'You shall not murder.' (Exodus 20:13 [NIV]) • Suffering can bring people closer to God and help them to understand Jesus' suffering.

A **Explain an argument** in favour of euthanasia and an argument against

B 'Euthanasia should be allowed.'

Give one view about this statement and support it with reasoned arguments and religious teaching.

TIP

You can use 'love your neighbour' in a discussion of euthanasia. However, to use it most effectively, consider to whom it is most loving and to whom it may not be loving.

RECAP

Essential information:

☐ Christians believe in life after death; they believe in the judgement of God and hope that they will be able to live with God after death.

☐ Christians believe that what people do on earth affects what happens to them after death.

Is death the end?

For a Christian, death is not the end but the beginning of something different. Atheists disagree but if Christians are correct, the afterlife applies to both believers and non-believers. Although there are differences in beliefs between Christians, they are summarised below.

- Christians believe God judges whether the deceased person spends **eternity** in heaven or hell. This means that, unlike life on earth, heaven and hell are never ending.
- Catholics believe in purgatory, where souls are purified to allow them to access God and heaven.
- Some Christians believe this process begins as soon as a person dies.
- Others believe that Jesus will return on a future day of judgement when all souls will be judged.
- Some believe that people will be in heaven in their physical bodies, others believe it is just their souls.
- Jesus' resurrection, referred to in John 11:25–26, is evidence that there is an afterlife.
- Some believe that God, who is the source of all good, would not condemn people to hell and that all go to heaven; others believe that all who go to hell deserve their fate.

What are heaven and hell like?

Heaven	Hell
• A wonderful place where God lives. • Revelation 4:2–6 describes a vision of God's throne room in heaven with everybody worshipping him. • Revelation 21:4 describes how there will be no more death, mourning or tears in heaven because the old order is replaced by the new one.	• Originally designed for Satan (the devil) and his fallen angels. • A blazing furnace with weeping and gnashing of teeth that exists to punish the unrighteous (Matthew 13:50). • An eternal place of torment where there is no rest (Revelation 14:11). 

- Although some Christians believe these descriptions to be literally true, others believe that hell symbolises the frustration of not being in the presence of God and the idea that it should be avoided.
- A more modern interpretation is that heaven is a state of being where God is present and hell a state of being without the possibility of God.

Eternity in heaven

Christians believe that heaven is not gained simply by being a good person, but is a free gift to those who believe and put their trust in Jesus. Many Christians believe that following Jesus still means living a life of doing good and avoiding sin, but salvation does not have to be earned.

> " Confess… "Jesus is Lord" and believe in your heart that God raised him from the dead. "
> *Romans 10:9* [NIV]

APPLY

A Explain **two** things a person has to do to be with God after death.

B 'There is no heaven or hell.'

Develop an argument that agrees with this statement. Try to include some religious content.

Test the 1 mark question

1 Which **one** of the following describes is euthanasia?

    A A type of abortion   B A method of animal testing

    C A good or gentle death   D A scientific view about the origin of the earth   **[1 mark]**

2 According to the Genesis creation story, which **one** of the following was created last?

    A Plants   B Humans   C Birds   D Fish and sea creatures   **[1 mark]**

Test the 2 mark question

3 Give **two** conditions which may lead to an abortion being allowed in the UK.   **[2 marks]**

    1) _____

    2) _____

4 Give **two** Christian beliefs about heaven.   **[2 marks]**

    1) _____

    2) _____

Test the 4 mark question

5 Explain **two** contrasting beliefs in contemporary British society about euthanasia. In your answer you should refer to the main religious tradition of Great Britain and one or more other religious traditions.   **[4 marks]**

● **Explain one belief.**	*Christians believe that life is God-given and sacred.*
● Develop your explanation with more detail/an example/ reference to a religious teaching or quotation.	*They believe in the sanctity of life, so ending life prematurely is not allowed because it is against God's plan for that person.*
● **Explain a second contrasting belief.**	*Many Hindus also disagree with euthanasia but for a different reason. They believe that suffering is a result of bad karma from a previous life.*
● Develop your explanation with more detail/an example/ reference to a religious teaching or quotation.	*Because of this, euthanasia is seen as trying to escape from the consequences of bad karma and this would badly affect the person's next life.*

TIP

In a 'contrasting' question, you don't necessarily need to give opposing viewpoints, but do make sure that the reasons given are very different.

6 Explain **two** similar religious beliefs about animal experimentation. In your answer, you must refer to one or more religious traditions.   **[4 marks]**

● **Explain one belief.**	
● Develop your explanation with more detail/an example/ reference to a religious teaching or quotation.	
● **Explain a second similar belief.**	
● Develop your explanation with more detail/an example/ reference to a religious teaching or quotation.	

7 Explain **two** contrasting religious beliefs about the use of natural resources.

In your answer, you must refer to one or more religious traditions.   **[4 marks]**

4 Exam practice

Test the 5 mark question

8   Explain **two** religious beliefs about what happens when a person dies.

Refer to sacred writings or another source of religious belief and teaching in your answer.   **[5 marks]**

● **Explain one belief.**	*Christians believe in the resurrection of the dead.*
● Develop your explanation with more detail/an example.	*Christians believe that the life and death of Jesus proves that there is life after death because he came back to life after being crucified, so those who believe in him can also have eternal life in heaven.*
● Add a reference to sacred writing or another source of religious belief and teaching. If you prefer, you can add this reference to your second belief instead.	*The Christian belief in resurrection is supported by the words of Jesus, "I am the resurrection and the life. He who believes in me will live, even though he dies; and whoever lives and believes in me will never die."*
● **Explain a second belief.**	*Sikhs believe in reincarnation.*
● Develop your explanation with more detail/an example.	*Sikhs believe what happens after death depends on the words spoken, the thoughts and deeds of the previous lifetime, or lifetimes.*

> **TIP**
> Here the reference to sacred writings follows the first belief. There is no need to include the exact Bible reference and doing so will not earn you any marks.

9   Explain **two** religious beliefs about the duty of human beings to protect the earth.

Refer to sacred writings or another source of religious belief and teaching in your answer.   **[5 marks]**

> **TIP**
> Make sure you read the whole question carefully. The word 'duty' here is an important one.

● **Explain one belief.**	
● Develop your explanation with more detail/an example.	
● **Explain a second belief.**	
● Develop your explanation with more detail/an example.	
● Add a reference to sacred writing or another source of religious belief and teaching. If you prefer, you can add this reference to your first belief instead.	

10   Explain **two** religious beliefs about the origins of the universe.

Refer to sacred writings or another source of religious belief and teaching in your answer.   **[5 marks]**

4 Exam practice

Test the 12 mark question

11 'Religious believers should not eat meat.'
    Evaluate this statement. In your answer you:
    - should give reasoned arguments in support of this statement
    - should give reasoned arguments to support a different point of view
    - should refer to religious arguments
    - may refer to non-religious arguments
    - should reach a justified conclusion.

[12 mark
Plus SPaG 3 ma

REASONED ARGUMENTS IN SUPPORT OF THE STATEMENT ● **Explain why some people would agree with the statement.** ● Develop your explanation with more detail and examples. ● Refer to religious teaching. Use a quote or paraphrase or refer to a religious authority. ● **Evaluate the arguments.** Is this a good argument or not? Explain why you think this.	*Eating meat involves the killing of animals to provide the meat. This is seen by many religious believers as cruel and unnecessary and they are quite happy to be vegetarians. For others, it is not just the killing of the animals that is the problem – the way they are treated throughout their short lives is much worse. Their death, so they can be used as meat, is often merciful because it ends their inhumane treatment. Some of the worst abuse happens to chickens who live their lives in cages in barns and never see daylight or breathe fresh air because they never leave their cage. This completely ignores the stewardship role humans have which means they should care for all living creatures. All living beings are valuable to God: 'not one of them is forgotten by God'.*
REASONED ARGUMENTS SUPPORTING A DIFFERENT VIEW ● **Explain why some people would support a different view.** ● Develop your explanation with more detail and examples. ● Refer to religious teaching. Use a quote or paraphrase or refer to a religious authority. ● **Evaluate the arguments.** Is this a good argument or not? Explain why you think this.	*Most Christians and Muslims do eat meat because they believe that it is a good source of protein. Although they believe that animals should not be treated cruelly, they believe that they were created by God for human use which includes killing them for food. As far as we know Jesus and Muhammad ate meat, and the fact that food laws are part of Islam and they make it clear how animals should be killed for meat means that Islam is in favour of meat eating.*
CONCLUSION ● **Give a justified conclusion.** ● Include your own opinion together with your own reasoning. ● **Include evaluation.** Explain why you think one viewpoint is stronger than the other or why they are equally strong. ● Do not just repeat arguments you have already used without explaining how they apply to your reasoned opinion/conclusion.	*So there is a difference of opinion concerning whether it is right to eat meat. Although I can see why some people prefer not to kill animals, I believe that meat is important for a balanced diet. Also many farmers would lose their livelihoods if people stopped eating meat. In my opinion it would be unfair on religious believers if they were prevented from enjoying meat. I can see that if your religion opposes meat eating then you would need to keep the rules of your faith. However, within Christianity this does not apply as God gave Noah permission to eat meat.*

TIP
This section about th treatment of animal shows an excellent cha of reasoning. It starts with an introductory statement, followed by development, an opinion and includes religion which is further elaborated.

TIP
Although there is good content in here, greater development about food laws in Islam would improve it, e.g further explanation about how animals are killed humanely.

TIP
This is a good conclusion because it includes reference to the arguments already made and supports them with more reasoning, not just the same as before.

12 'The law on abortion should be changed to allow more abortions.'

Evaluate this statement. In your answer you:

- should give reasoned arguments in support of this statement
- should give reasoned arguments to support a different point of view
- should refer to religious arguments
- may refer to non-religious arguments
- should reach a justified conclusion.

TIP

Make sure you focus on whether the law should be changed, not just on whether abortion is right or wrong.

[12 marks]
Plus SPaG 3 marks

REASONED ARGUMENTS IN SUPPORT OF THE STATEMENT ● **Explain why some people would agree with the statement.** ● Develop your explanation with more detail and examples. ● Refer to religious teaching. Use a quote or paraphrase or refer to a religious authority. ● **Evaluate the arguments.** Is this a good argument or not? Explain why you think this.	
REASONED ARGUMENTS SUPPORTING A DIFFERENT VIEW ● **Explain why some people would support a different view.** ● Develop your explanation with more detail and examples. ● Refer to religious teaching. Use a quote or paraphrase or refer to a religious authority. ● **Evaluate the arguments.** Is this a good argument or not? Explain why you think this.	
CONCLUSION ● **Give a justified conclusion.** ● Include your own opinion together with your own reasoning. ● **Include evaluation.** Explain why you think one viewpoint is stronger than the other or why they are equally strong. ● Do not just repeat arguments you have already used without explaining how they apply to your reasoned opinion/conclusion.	

13 'Humans should use the earth's resources however they wish.'

Evaluate this statement. In your answer you:

- should give reasoned arguments in support of this statement
- should give reasoned arguments to support a different point of view
- should refer to religious arguments
- may refer to non-religious arguments
- should reach a justified conclusion.

[12 marks]
Plus SPaG 3 marks

Check your answers using the mark scheme on page 124. How did you do?
To feel more secure in the content you need to remember, re-read pages 58–65.
To remind yourself of what the examiner is looking for, go to pages 6–11.

5.1 The Design argument

RECAP

Essential information:

☐ The **Design argument** says that because everything is so intricately made, it must have been created by God.

Did God create the universe?

- Christians are **theists** (people who believe in God) and they believe that God planned and created the earth.
- He created it for a purpose and put living things on it, including humans.
- Because everything is so intricate and complex and works well together God must have planned what he made.
- It cannot be a product of chance so it must have been designed.
- **Atheists**, who don't believe in God, believe the universe was not created, but evolved naturally. An **agnostic** believes there is not enough evidence that God exists or that he created the universe.

> **TIP**
> See pages 58 and 62 for more about the origins of the universe and human life.

Some different Design arguments

William Paley	Isaac Newton	Thomas Aquinas	F. R. Tennant
Paley (1743–1805) argued that, if someone found a watch and did not know what it was, its workings are so intricate that they would believe they must have been designed and made by a watchmaker. It could not be accidental. Similarly, the universe is so complex and intricate that it must have been designed and made, and the only possibility is that it was the work of God.	Newton (1642–1726) argued that the 'opposable thumb' that humans and some primates have allows precise and delicate movement and allows humans to do such things as tying a shoelace or writing with a pen. This is sufficient evidence of design which can only have been achieved by God.	In the thirteenth century, Aquinas stated that only an intelligent being could keep everything in the universe in regular order. The fact the planets rotate in the solar system without colliding is because of God.	In the 1930s, Tennant said that since everything was just right for humans to develop, the world must have been designed by God. He referred to the strength of gravity being absolutely right and said that if the force and speed of the explosion caused by the Big Bang was slightly different, life could not have developed on earth.

Objections to the Design arguments

- Natural selection happens by chance. The fact that the fittest survive and the rest die out is pure chance. Species design themselves through the process of evolution not through a designer God.
- The amount of suffering in the world proves there is no designer God because a good God would not have designed and allowed bad things, such as natural disasters and evil.
- The order in the universe, necessary to support life, makes it look as though it is designed when in fact the order and structure in nature is imposed by humans.

APPLY

(A) Choose **two** of the arguments for the design of the universe and write down their main points.

(B) 'The Design argument proves that God exists.'

Write two developed arguments, one in agreement and one against this statement.

Essential information:

☐ The **First Cause argument** states that there has to be an uncaused cause that made everything else happen.

The First Cause argument

The logical chain of reasoning for the First Cause argument runs like this:

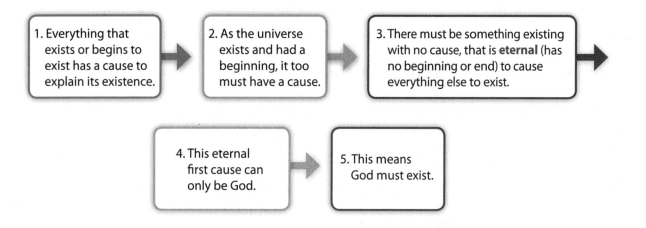

1. Everything that exists or begins to exist has a cause to explain its existence.

2. As the universe exists and had a beginning, it too must have a cause.

3. There must be something existing with no cause, that is **eternal** (has no beginning or end) to cause everything else to exist.

4. This eternal first cause can only be God.

5. This means God must exist.

- The First Cause or Cosmological argument relies on the belief that **the universe had a beginning and a cause**.
- Most scientists accept that **the universe began as a result of the Big Bang**.
- Christians and other theists might accept the Big Bang theory, **but would argue that God was the cause of the Big Bang**.

Thomas Aquinas' First Cause argument

In the thirteenth century, Thomas Aquinas argued that everything in the universe is caused to exist. Nothing can become something by itself. Since nothing we observe can cause itself to exist, there are only two possibilities:

- an infinite chain of events preceded by causes or
- a first cause that itself is uncaused by anything else.

Since an infinite chain of causes and effects is impossible, because it would take an infinite amount of time to reach us, there must have been a first cause. Aquinas believed this first cause to be God.

Objections to the First Cause argument

- Atheists argue that if everything that exists has a cause, who or what caused God?
- Surely if God is eternal the universe can be eternal as well.
- The idea that everything has a cause does not necessarily mean the universe has to have a cause as well.
- The Big Bang was a random event and had nothing to do with God.
- Religious **creation** stories, about how God brought the universe into being, such as the one in Genesis, are myths. The truth they tell is spiritual, not actual.

A Explain carefully **two** of the arguments included in the First Cause argument.

B 'The First Cause argument proves that God exists.'

Write two developed arguments, one in agreement and one against the statement.

> TIP
>
> The five-point logical chain of reasoning gives a simple overview of the First Cause argument.

Essential information:

☐ The argument from miracles tries to prove that God exists, but it has strengths and weaknesses.

☐ There are contrasting beliefs about miracles from Christian and non-religious perspectives.

What is a miracle?

A **miracle** is a seemingly impossible event, usually good, that cannot be explained by natural or scientific laws. Christians believe a true miracle is an event performed by God. Examples include recovering from an illness when doctors had given up hope and avoiding certain death from a freak accident.

Theists believe that through these events God shows his love and a believer's faith may be strengthened.

The argument from miracles and objections to it

Christians and other theists argue that:
- There is no scientific reason for an event happening so it must be caused by something outside nature.
- God is the only thing that exists outside nature.
- These events must be the result of God's intervention in the world.
- **Therefore God must exist.**

Atheists and agnostics may argue that:
- Miracles are no more than happy coincidences.
- They may be explained by scientific explanations not yet discovered
- Healings could be the result of mind over matter or wrongly diagnosed illnesses.
- Some miracles are deliberately made up for fame or money.
- **Therefore what appear to be miracles have nothing to do with God, so they cannot prove God exists.**

David Hume, a philosopher in the eighteenth century, argued against miracles:

- Miracles deny the laws of nature but there can never be enough evidence to prove this can happen.
- Witnesses to miracles are unreliable, as most of them are uneducated, primitive people.
- Religions depend on miracles to prove they are true but all religions cannot be right.

Some theists also deny the truth of miracles. They ask why God chooses someone to benefit from a miracle over millions who are not so fortunate. An all-just and all-loving God wouldn't do that.

You might be asked to compare beliefs on the argument from miracles between Christianity (the main religious tradition in Great Britain) and another religious tradition.

Christian responses

Christians view miracles as evidence of God's existence and work in the world.

- Jesus worked many miracles, e.g. healings, bringing the dead back to life.
- Jesus' incarnation and resurrection are considered the most important miracles in Christian teaching.
- Lourdes is recognised by the Church as a place where miracles have occurred – the Catholic Church has recorded 69 miracles there.
- The fact that some people convert to Christianity after experiencing a miracle is seen as proof of God's existence.

A Explain carefully how some Christians use miracles to prove the existence of God.

B **Finish this sentence** with a detailed explanation, then write a detailed explanation of a different point of view.

"When David Hume argued against miracles I believe he was right because..."

Essential information:

☐ Some use science and the existence of suffering and evil to challenge the existence of God.

☐ For some theists the Design argument, First Cause and the argument from miracles do not provide **proof** (evidence that supports the truth of something) that God exists, but they strengthen the **faith** (their commitment to God that goes beyond proof) that they already have in God.

How science is used to challenge belief in God

- Some atheists believe that religious beliefs, especially about God, were invented by people in the past to answer questions about the origins of the universe. Similarly questions about hardship, such as the failure of crops, could best be explained as punishment from God.
- Science can now answer these questions and in the future, science will be able to answer all currently unanswered questions, so atheists argue that the invented idea of God is no longer necessary or helpful.
- The fact that science is getting closer to creating human life provides further evidence that God does not exist.

Many Christians see no conflict between science and religion. They understand science as explaining the continuing process that God used when creating the universe. However fundamentalist Christians would argue that you shouldn't change religious truths to fit scientific laws. Doing this puts other religious teaching in doubt.

> **❝**The big bang [...] does not contradict the divine act of creation; rather, it requires it [...] He [God] created beings and let them develop according to internal laws which he gave every one.**❞**
> *Pope Francis, speaking at the Pontifical Academy of Sciences, 2014*

Evil and suffering as an argument against the existence of God

Atheists argue that the existence of **evil** (a force of negative power) and **suffering** (the unpleasant conditions people sometimes have to live with) show that God does not exist. They may also say that if God designed the world, he didn't do it very well. They use natural disasters and the cruelty in parts of the animal world as evidence for this.

Their arguments follow a logical sequence:

| 1. God is believed to be all-knowing, all-powerful and all-loving. | → | 2. If this is true, God should be aware of evil and use his powers to prevent it because he loves his creation. | → | 3. God doesn't do this, so he doesn't exist. |

- Christians argue that suffering and evil is the result of free will. God gave humans the ability to choose what they do and this gives them power to make wrong choices.
- Adam and Eve's disobedience brought evil and suffering into God's perfect world.
- If there was no good and bad in the world, people would not be able to show their human qualities to the full, for example, by demonstrating compassion.

A Explain **two** reasons why atheists may believe that evil and suffering proves God doesn't exist and **two** ways that Christians counter their reasoning.

B Write **two** logical chains of reasoning, one to agree that science challenges the existence of God and the other to disagree.

> **TIP**
> Remember that a logical chain of reasoning can express an opinion, give a reason to support the opinion and further develop the reason, possibly using religious arguments to elaborate it.

RECAP

Essential information:

☐ **Special revelation** is God making himself known through direct personal experience or an unusual specific event.

☐ **Enlightenment** is gaining true knowledge about God, usually through meditation and self-discipline.

☐ Special revelation and enlightenment are both sources of knowledge about the divine.

What is meant by divine?

All religions believe that there is a supreme, final fundamental power in all reality (**ultimate reality**) which is eternal and unchanging. It could be a God or gods which are referred to as being **divine**. Christians believe that the ultimate reality is a personal being, God, who makes himself known in three persons: Father, Son and Holy Spirit.

Special revelation

- Some theists say that God cannot be known because he is beyond the limits of human understanding and cannot be described in language.
- Christians accept that they cannot fully understand God, but believe that they can know something of his nature and purpose through revelations.
- Special revelation is the term given to a person experiencing God directly in a particular event. It usually has a profound effect on those directly involved and can be life changing.
- Examples from the Bible include Moses receiving the Ten Commandments from God or Mary finding out she was to give birth to Jesus.

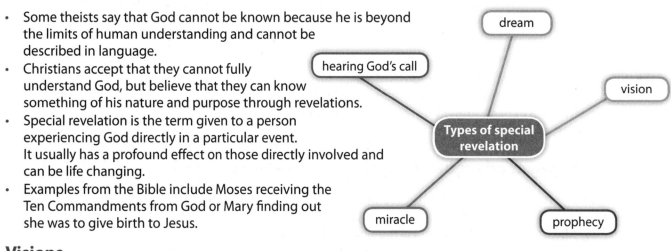

dream

hearing God's call

vision

Types of special revelation

miracle

prophecy

Visions

Visions involve seeing something that shows something about the nature of God. Visions often involve seeing holy figures, but some atheists believe they can be explained by sleep deprivation or drug use.

Examples of visions in the Bible include Isaiah 6:1–10 and Saul's vision on the Damascus Road in Acts 9:1–19. Saul was bringing followers of Jesus who had been spreading his message back to Jerusalem for trial and sentence. He experienced a blinding light and was spoken to by Jesus. Afterwards he changed his name to Paul, was baptised as a Christian and committed himself to the Christian faith – a faith whose followers he had previously persecuted. He spent the rest of his life spreading the message of Christianity throughout the Roman Empire.

> You might be asked to compare beliefs on visions between Christianity, the main religious tradition in Great Britain, and another religious tradition.

Enlightenment

Buddhists do not believe in God or gods. However, they use meditation and self-discipline to discover the meaning of ultimate reality by gaining true knowledge (enlightenment). They hope to discover how to end suffering and achieve happiness by escaping the cycle of birth, death and rebirth.

APPLY

(A) Using **one** detailed example, explain the meaning of special revelation.

(B) 'Those who see visions are only hallucinating.'

Write a detailed argument that shows what you think about this statement.

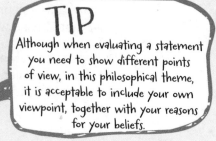

TIP

Although when evaluating a statement you need to show different points of view, in this philosophical theme, it is acceptable to include your own viewpoint, together with your reasons for your beliefs.

Essential information:

Some seek to understand the divine by using **general revelation** (God making himself known through ordinary experiences), through **nature** (the physical world) and **scripture** (the sacred writings of a religion).

What is general revelation?

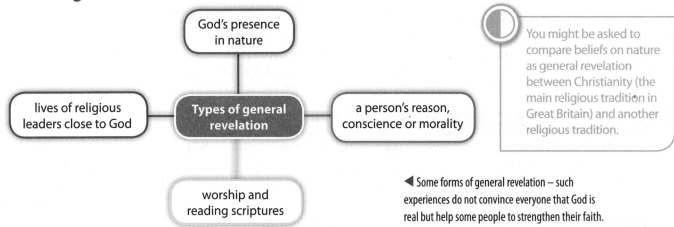

God's presence in nature

lives of religious leaders close to God

Types of general revelation

a person's reason, conscience or morality

worship and reading scriptures

You might be asked to compare beliefs on nature as general revelation between Christianity (the main religious tradition in Great Britain) and another religious tradition.

◀ Some forms of general revelation – such experiences do not convince everyone that God is real but help some people to strengthen their faith.

Nature as a way of understanding the divine

- Many Christians believe that God is revealed to them through the beauty of the world (the power of storms and the sea, the wonder of a newborn baby, etc.). This leads to awe and wonder at his power to create and destroy.
- Atheists or humanists may argue that observing nature does not provide a greater understanding of God, but can lead to greater scientific truth.

> ❝The heavens declare the glory of God; the skies proclaim the work of his hands …
> night after night they reveal knowledge.❞
> *Psalm 19:1–2 [NIV]*

Scripture as a way of understanding the divine

For Christians, the word scripture means the writings in the Bible. It describes how God acted in the past and he is revealed as powerful, just, loving and forgiving.

There are different ways to approach scripture.

Literal interpretation	Liberal interpretation	Atheist interpretation
The Bible contains God's actual words.	The Bible was inspired by God and can be interpreted in different ways.	The writings in the Bible are merely the authors' opinions.
The words must not be changed or questioned.	The words must be seen in their original context and understood differently in today's world.	The words of the Bible do not reveal anything about God.

Although what the Bible teaches about God cannot be proved, the writings of the Bible show a deep human awareness of the nature of God. When Christians read or listen to the words of the Bible, they hope to get a better understanding of the teachings of Christianity and to receive spiritual strength from God's words.

APPLY

(A) Explain **two** ways in which Christians believe general revelation helps them to understand God.

(B) **Complete this developed point** about whether the Bible can help people to believe in God.

"It is impossible to believe that an ancient book can help people to believe in God. It was written such a long time ago."

> TIP
> Developing your personal belief and arguments to support it may improve your answer, but don't forget that in the 12 mark question you have to give an alternative point of view as well and support it.

RECAP

Essential information:

☐ Although it is difficult to describe the infinite, unseen God, many ideas about God come from revelation.

☐ There are different ideas about qualities of the divine such as being omnipotent, omniscient, benevolent, personal, impersonal, immanent and transcendent.

Descriptions of God's nature

The limitations of language make describing a God without limits very difficult. However all of the major religions, apart from Buddhism, believe in one God who is creator, controller and maintainer of the universe. The table explains the main words used to describe God and his nature.

Description	Explanation
omnipotent	Almighty and all-powerful; capable of doing anything including creation.
omniscient	All-knowing and aware of everything that has happened in the past, present or future.
benevolent	All-loving and all-good – provider of everything humans need to survive.
personal	The idea that God has 'human' characteristics, such as being merciful and compassionate. Humans can have a relationship with God through prayer.
impersonal	The idea that God has no 'human' characteristics, is unknowable and mysterious and more like an idea or a force.
immanent	A belief that God is present in, and involved with, life in the universe. People can experience God in their lives as he influences events.
transcendent	A belief that God is beyond and outside life on earth. He is not limited by the world, time or space.

> **TIP**
> As all of these terms are listed in the specification, you may need to know about any or all of them.

> ❝You have searched me LORD, and you know me. You know when I sit and when I rise; you perceive my thoughts from afar. ❞
>
> *Psalm 139:1–2 [NIV]*

Can God be immanent and transcendent, personal and impersonal?

Even though they appear to be opposites, some Christians believe that for them, God is both immanent and personal and transcendent and impersonal. God is a mystery beyond human understanding.

- God's immanence is revealed both in Jesus, who they believe is God made man and also in the work of the Holy Spirit.
- However, he must also be transcendent as creator of the universe. Nothing would exist without God.
- God is also personal because he allows followers to join in a relationship with him, described as a Father who loves and cares for his children. This relationship is enabled by prayer.
- However, despite this, he can also be an impersonal force or power.

These seemingly contradictory roles would not be possible for anyone other than God, who is believed to be without limits.

APPLY

(A) For the **seven** ideas about the divine, design and draw a simple symbol to help you remember them.

> **TIP**
> Even though a quotation such as this has a specific religious theme, don't forget to include specific religious content in your answer.

(B) 'No being can have the qualities and nature that Christians believe God has.'

Write two developed points of view about this, one in favour and one that expresses a different opinion.

5.8 The value of revelation and enlightenment

Essential information:

☐ Theists believe that revelation and enlightenment are sources of knowledge about the divine.

☐ Some people find it difficult to accept the reality in some examples of revelation.

The value of revelation

For theists revelation can:

- provide proof of God's existence
- help to start a religion
- enable believers to have a relationship with the divine
- help people know how God wants them to live.

Christians believe that revelation can come through the work and example of 'ordinary people' who may not be aware that they have provided a revelation. Revelation is not just given to those in a position of responsibility within a faith.

Revelation: reality or illusion?

Revelation cannot be proved, so how do believers know it is real? They may ask themselves:

Question	Christian responses
Does their revelation match the real world?	It is probably unlikely if it claims that people can fly. If it claims that water in a holy place can cure, and it does, then it is more likely to be a real revelation.
Does it fit with other revelations acknowledged to be correct in a religion?	If it contradicts the long-held belief of a religion, it is less likely to be a true revelation. However, beliefs may change over time so this is not always the case.
Does it change a non-believer into a believer, or convert someone from one religion to another?	Nicky Cruz, a gang leader in New York in the 1950s, was converted to Christianity through the teaching of a Christian street preacher called David Wilkerson, whose words and example came as a revelation to Cruz.
How is it that different religions have different revelations? They can't all be correct.	Different religions are different paths to the divine chosen by different people. Within a faith there are different interpretations, such as whether Christians should favour the death penalty. Both sides can use the Bible as evidence.

Alternative explanations for the experiences

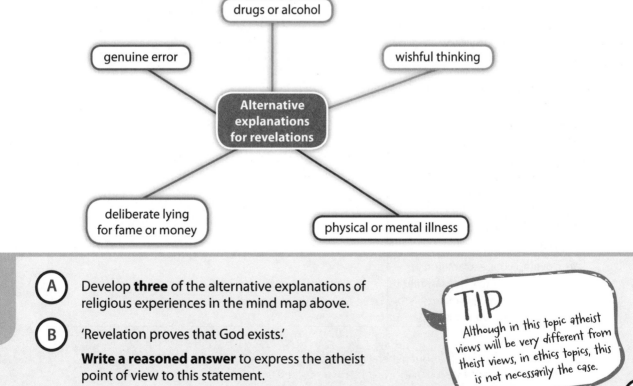

A Develop **three** of the alternative explanations of religious experiences in the mind map above.

B 'Revelation proves that God exists.'

Write a reasoned answer to express the atheist point of view to this statement.

TIP
Although in this topic atheist views will be very different from theist views, in ethics topics, this is not necessarily the case.

5 Exam practice

Test the 1 mark question

1. Which **one** of the following describes a person who believes in God?

   A Atheist   B Agnostic   C Theist   D Humanist   **[1 mark]**

2. Which **one** of the following is **not** an attribute of God?

   A Compassionate   B Mortal   C Transcendent   D Eternal   **[1 mark]**

Test the 2 mark question

3. Give **two** weaknesses of the First Cause argument.   **[2 marks]**

   1) _____

   2) _____

4. Give **two** possible causes of suffering.   **[2 marks]**

   1) _____

   2) _____

Test the 4 mark question

5. Explain **two** contrasting beliefs in contemporary British society about the Design argument for God's existence.

   In your answer you must refer to one or more religious traditions. You may refer to a non-religious belief.   **[4 marks]**

● **Explain one belief.**	*Christians believe that the beauty and intricacy of nature proves that God created the world.*
● Develop your explanation with more detail/an example/ reference to a religious teaching or quotation.	*William Paley said that just as a watch's intricate workings show evidence of design, so does the universe, which is more complex than a watch.*
● **Explain a second contrasting belief.**	*Atheists disagree with the Design argument because they do not believe there is a God.*
● Develop your explanation with more detail/an example/ reference to a religious teaching or quotation.	*They think that the natural world evolved after the Big Bang, a random event, and through natural selection creatures designed themselves without a need for God.*

   > **TIP**
   >
   > Remember 'contrasti[ng] means different. He[re] the answer refers t[o] Christianity and contr[asts] it with an atheist vie[w].

6. Explain **two** contrasting beliefs about miracles.   **[4 marks]**

● **Explain one belief.**	
● Develop your explanation with more detail/an example/ reference to a religious teaching or quotation.	
● **Explain a second contrasting belief.**	
● Develop your explanation with more detail/an example/ reference to a religious teaching or quotation.	

7. Explain **two** similar beliefs about general revelation.   **[4 marks]**

Test the 5 mark question

8 Explain **two** religious beliefs about visions.

Refer to sacred writings or another source of religious belief and teaching in your answer. **[5 marks]**

● **Explain one belief.**	*Christians believe that God can be revealed to people in a special, direct way through visions.*
● Develop your explanation with more detail/an example.	*Some people who have had visions may as a result have a dramatic conversion from one way of life or faith to another.*
● **Explain a second belief.**	*A second Christian belief about visions is that they reveal a message to a person which makes them want to spread the word of God to other people.*
● Develop your explanation with more detail/an example.	*Since they believe the vision was given for a specific purpose, they often begin a life of preaching or sharing their experiences with others.*
● Add a reference to sacred writings or another source of religious belief and teaching. If you prefer, you can add this reference to your first belief instead.	*An example of a vision in the Bible is in Acts 9:1–19, where it says Saul (who later became Paul) received a vision of Jesus on the Damascus Road. Saul was temporarily blinded and when he regained his sight he changed from persecuting Christians to preaching the gospel of Jesus to everyone.*

TIP
The reference to Saul's conversion is longer than necessary but certainly gains the mark for referring to sacred writings.

9 Explain **two** religious beliefs about special revelation.

Refer to sacred writings or another source of religious belief and teaching in your answer. **[5 marks]**

● **Explain one belief.**	
● Develop your explanation with more detail/an example.	
● **Explain a second belief.**	
● Develop your explanation with more detail/an example.	
● Add a reference to sacred writings or another source of religious belief and teaching. If you prefer, you can add this reference to your first belief instead.	

TIP
Make sure you write about special revelation, **not** general revelation.

TIP
This question is not an evaluation, so do **not** give your opinion or write arguments against revelation. Don't forget to include a source of religious teaching in the answer.

10 Explain **two** religious ideas about God.

Refer to sacred writings or another source of religious belief and teaching in your answer. **[5 marks]**

Test the 12 mark question

11   'The First Cause argument proves that God exists.'

Evaluate this statement. In your answer you:

- should give reasoned arguments in support of this statement
- should give reasoned arguments to support a different point of view
- should refer to religious arguments
- may refer to non-religious arguments
- should reach a justified conclusion.

[12 mark

Plus SPaG 3 ma

REASONED ARGUMENTS IN SUPPORT OF THE STATEMENT ● **Explain why some people would agree with the statement.** ● Develop your explanation with more detail and examples. ● Refer to religious teaching. Use a quote or paraphrase or refer to a religious authority. ● **Evaluate the arguments.** Is this a good argument or not? Explain why you think this.	*The First Cause argument says that everything that exists has a cause. It is obvious to everyone that the universe exists because we live in it! Therefore the universe, too, must have a cause – something must have started it. But that something had to be eternal and not caused by something else, otherwise that other thing would be the cause, and so on. Christians believe that God is the eternal, almighty cause that began the process of creation of everything we know. The Bible says that God merely said, 'Let there be light' and it was created. So God was the eternal being that set off the Big Bang which led to evolution and the world as we know it today.*
REASONED ARGUMENTS SUPPORTING A DIFFERENT VIEW ● **Explain why some people would support a different view.** ● Develop your explanation with more detail and examples. ● Refer to religious teaching. Use a quote or paraphrase or refer to a religious authority. ● **Evaluate the arguments.** Is this a good argument or not? Explain why you think this.	*Atheists are people who do not believe there is a God. They would argue that the First Cause argument does not prove there is a God because there are flaws in the logic – the argument contradicts itself. For example, if everything has a cause, what caused God? They also point out that saying God is eternal, so nobody made him, is just a convenient excuse. If God is eternal, why cannot the universe be eternal? Of course, if the universe is eternal, it doesn't need a first cause and was never created. This then removes the need for a God to cause the universe to exist. They also point out that the Big Bang just happened and there was no cause for it.*
CONCLUSION ● **Give a justified conclusion.** ● Include your own opinion together with your own reasoning. ● **Include evaluation.** Explain why you think one viewpoint is stronger than the other or why they are equally strong. ● Do not just repeat arguments you have already used without explaining how they apply to your reasoned opinion/conclusion.	*In conclusion, I think that although the First Cause argument may seem convincing because it depends on something everyone can observe, that everything that happens has a cause, in the end it fails to convince me that a God is the First Cause of the universe. The argument relies on the universe having a beginning and a cause, but just because things in our world have causes does not necessarily mean the universe itself had one. Christians may use the Bible's creation stories to support their arguments in favour of the statement, but as I am an atheist, I am not persuaded by myths.*

TIP

It is good to mention the B
Bang here, and it links well to
previous argument. This poin
could be developed further,
perhaps with a brief explanati
of the Big Bang theory and
some evaluation as to how
convincing it is.

TIP

This conclusion is good
because it doesn't just
repeat points already
made to justify the
opinion. It is also clearl
linked to the statemen
in the question.

12 'Miracles prove that God exists.'

Evaluate this statement. In your answer you:
- should give reasoned arguments in support of this statement
- should give reasoned arguments to support a different point of view
- should refer to religious arguments
- may refer to non-religious arguments
- should reach a justified conclusion.

[12 marks]

Plus SPaG 3 marks

REASONED ARGUMENTS IN SUPPORT OF THE STATEMENT ● **Explain why some people would agree with the statement.** ● Develop your explanation with more detail and examples. ● Refer to religious teaching. Use a quote or paraphrase or refer to a religious authority. ● **Evaluate the arguments.** Is this a good argument or not? Explain why you think this.	
REASONED ARGUMENTS SUPPORTING A DIFFERENT VIEW ● **Explain why some people would support a different view.** ● Develop your explanation with more detail and examples. ● Refer to religious teaching. Use a quote or paraphrase or refer to a religious authority. ● **Evaluate the arguments.** Is this a good argument or not? Explain why you think this.	
CONCLUSION ● **Give a justified conclusion.** ● Include your own opinion together with your own reasoning. ● **Include evaluation.** Explain why you think one viewpoint is stronger than the other or why they are equally strong. ● Do not just repeat arguments you have already used without explaining how they apply to your reasoned opinion/conclusion.	

TIP

Make sure your focus is on both miracles and the existence of God.

13 'The existence of evil and suffering proves that God does not exist.'

Evaluate this statement. In your answer you:
- should give reasoned arguments in support of this statement
- should give reasoned arguments to support a different point of view
- should refer to religious arguments
- may refer to non-religious arguments
- should reach a justified conclusion.

[12 marks]

Plus SPaG 3 marks

Check your answers using the mark scheme on page 124. How did you do?
To feel more secure in the content you need to remember, re-read pages 70–77.
To remind yourself of what the examiner is looking for, go to pages 6–11.

6.1 Introduction to religion, peace and conflict

RECAP

Essential information:

☐ Throughout history people have gone to **war** (fighting between nations to resolve differences between them). Often the intention of those fighting a war is to create **peace**, an absence of conflict, which leads to happiness and harmony.

☐ Many wars are fought to achieve **justice** (bringing about what is right and fair, according to the law, or making up for a wrong that has been committed). Christians believe that after a war **forgiveness** (pardoning someone for wrongdoing) and **reconciliation** (restoring friendly relationships after conflict) should follow.

☐ The concepts of peace, justice, forgiveness and reconciliation are important both in the aftermath of a conflict and as tools to prevent war happening in the first place.

Christian beliefs

- Christianity teaches that killing is wrong but many Christians have been prepared to fight for their faith or their country.
- Some Christians, e.g. Quakers (a Christian denomination committed to pacifism), believe war is always wrong and they work to prevent it.

Peace
• The aim of war may be peace but this may be hard to achieve because of the instability and resentment left after a war.
• Peace is also a feeling of happiness and tranquillity that can come through prayer and meditation which helps people to avoid conflict.
• The prophet Isaiah spoke of a time when God will bring peace.

> ❝He will judge between the nations and will settle disputes for many peoples… Nation will not take up sword against nation, nor will they train for war any more.❞
> *Isaiah 2:4* [NIV]

> ❝We are in the process of winning the war. We also have to win the peace. And winning the peace involves a whole series of acts to help democracy and development.❞
> *Laurent Fabius discussing conflict and reconciliation between France and Mali.*

Justice	Forgiveness	Reconciliation
• Isaiah says God, the ultimate judge, will establish justice.	• Christians are taught to forgive others if they wish to be forgiven (the Lord's Prayer).	• Reconciliation means a conscious effort to rebuild the relationship which has been damaged by conflict.
• Justice is linked to equality of opportunity.	• Forgiveness does not mean no action should be taken to right a wrong, but when conflict is over forgiveness should follow.	• It is also important in the prevention of conflict.
• If more privileged parts of the world are seen to be the cause of injustice, conflict may result.	• God offers forgiveness to all who ask in faith.	

APPLY

A **Develop** this point about forgiveness by explaining it in more detail or adding an example, and by referring to sacred writings or another source of religious belief and teaching in your answer.

"Christians have a duty to forgive others if they wish to be forgiven."

B Make a list of **three** arguments for and **three** arguments against the statement, 'Christians should not take part in wars.'

RECAP

Essential information:

☐ The right to **protest** (express disapproval, often in a public group) is a fundamental democratic freedom.

☐ UK law allows peaceful public protest marches if police are told six days before so that **violence** (actions that threaten or harm others) can be avoided.

☐ **Terrorism** (the unlawful use of violence, usually against innocent civilians, to achieve a political goal) is a more serious form of violent protest.

Violence and protest

- An unplanned protest can sometimes turn violent and cause riots.
- Christians believe that protest to achieve what is right is acceptable as long as violence is not used.
- The Christian pastor Dr Martin Luther King Jr organised peaceful protests against unjust racist laws, which succeeded in bringing civil rights to African American citizens.
- No religion promotes violence in their teachings and all religions teach that conflict should be avoided, but they have different views about when violence may be justified.

> You might be asked to compare beliefs on violence between Christianity (the main religious tradition in Great Britain) and another religious tradition.

Terrorism

- Some individuals or groups use terrorism to further their cause by killing innocent people.
- Suicide bombers, car bombs, gunmen shooting into crowds, using vehicles to injure pedestrians are all tactics of terrorism.
- The aim of terrorism is to make society aware of their cause, make people frightened and push the authorities into giving way to their demands.
- Terrorists may link their cause with a religion, including Christianity, but no religion promotes terrorism.
- Christians believe terrorism is wrong as it targets innocent people.

> ❝ The purpose of terrorism lies not just in the violent act itself. It is in producing terror. It sets out to inflame, to divide, to produce consequences which [terrorists] then use to justify terror. ❞
>
> *Former UK Prime Minister, Tony Blair.*

APPLY

(A) Give **two** reasons why Christians may wish to protest.

(B) **Develop** the following argument to support the statement, 'Terrorism is never justified' by explaining in more detail, adding an example, or referring to a relevant religious teaching or quotation.

"Terrorism kills innocent people. It uses violence to frighten and intimidate ordinary citizens who are just going about their daily lives. It can never be justified no matter what the cause."

6.3 Reasons for war

RECAP

Essential information:

Some reasons for war include:

- **greed** (selfish desire for something)
- **self-defence** (acting to prevent harm to yourself or others)
- **retaliation** (deliberately harming someone as a response to them harming you).

> **TIP**
> Other reasons for war such as political disputes, government change, clash of cultures or disputes between ethnic groups within a nation can be included in your answers on this topic.

Reasons for war

Greed	Self-defence	Retaliation
• To gain more land/regain land previously lost • To control important resources, e.g. oil • To deprive enemy of their main source of income	• To defend one's country against invasion or attack/ defend allies who are under threat • To defend one's values, beliefs and ways of life • To defeat evil, e.g. genocide (deliberate killing of a whole nation or ethnic group)	• To fight against a country that has done something very wrong • To fight against a country which has attacked or damaged your country

Christian beliefs

- The Bible warns against greed:

> **"** For the love of money is the root of all kinds of evil. Some people, eager for money, have wandered from the faith and pierced themselves with many griefs. **"**
> *1 Timothy 6:10 [NIV]*

- There is little to justify self-defence in the New Testament, but an argument could be made if all other ways of resolving conflict have been tried and failed.

> **"** Do not repay anyone evil for evil… If it is possible, as far as it depends on you, live at peace with everyone. **"**
> *Romans 12:17–19 [NIV]*

- Jesus taught that retaliation was wrong:

> **"** But I tell you, do not resist an evil person. If anyone slaps you on the right cheek, turn to them the other cheek also. **"**
> *Matthew 5:39 [NIV]*

- Many Christians can follow this advice in day-to-day interactions, but find it more difficult in situations of war.

APPLY

A Which one of the following is **not** a reason for war?

a) Self-defence   b) Greed   c) Retaliation   d) Forgiveness

B Use the table below with arguments for and against the statement, 'Retaliation is a justifiable reason for war.' **Write a paragraph** to explain whether you agree or disagree with the statement, having evaluated both sides of the argument.

For	Against
If a country has attacked you for no reason, you have every right to get back at them by harming them. They started the conflict so should expect a response.	Retaliation is wrong because it is just getting back at someone, which is likely to prolong the conflict rather than settle it. Jesus taught that retaliation is wrong when he told people to 'turn the other cheek'.
The Bible teaches 'An eye for an eye, a tooth for a tooth' so you should be able to retaliate when an enemy causes you harm. It's a matter of justice, which is an important principle.	Retaliation is different from self-defence. It is acceptable to defend your country but retaliation is a kind of spiteful action, taken to punish the enemy for something they've done. Jesus taught forgiveness and reconciliation to bring about peace.

RECAP

Essential information:

☐ **Nuclear weapons** are weapons that work by a nuclear reaction; they devastate huge areas and kill large numbers of people.

☐ **Weapons of mass destruction** (that kill large numbers of people/cause great damage) include:

- **chemical weapons** which use chemicals to poison, burn or paralyse humans and destroy the natural environment
- **biological weapons** which have living organisms or infective material that can lead to disease or death.

☐ No religion supports the use of these weapons.

The use of nuclear weapons

- US forces used atom bombs on Hiroshima and Nagasaki during the Second World War causing 140,000 people to die in Hiroshima alone.
- Japan surrendered, ending the war.
- Some people say their use ended the war so was justified.
- Since then many countries have developed powerful nuclear weapons as a deterrent (to prevent an enemy attack).

> **❝** Faith groups in the UK are united in their conviction that any use of nuclear weapons would violate the sanctity of life and the principle of dignity core to our faith traditions. **❞**
>
> *Steve Hucklesby*

Weapons of mass destruction

- The Chemical Weapons Convention (1993) made the production, stockpiling and use of these weapons illegal worldwide.
- Chemical weapons are thought to have been used in Iraq and Syria.
- Biological weapons introduce harmful bacteria and viruses into the atmosphere, food or water supplies that can kill large numbers of people.
- Biological weapons are illegal but many countries have them.

You might be asked to compare beliefs on weapons of mass destruction between Christianity (the main religious tradition in Great Britain) and another religious tradition.

Christian beliefs

- Only God has the right to end life.
- Nuclear, chemical and biological weapons kill huge numbers of innocent civilians so their use can never be justified.

> **❝** You shall not murder. **❞**
> *Exodus 20:13 [NIV]*

- Some Christians have used the idea of 'eye for eye, tooth for tooth' (Exodus 21:24) to justify war, but this cannot justify the use of weapons of mass destruction.
- Some Christians see nuclear weapons as a deterrent to maintain peace and prevent attack.

APPLY

(A) Explain **two** contrasting beliefs in contemporary British society about weapons of mass destruction. In your answer you should refer to the main religious tradition of Great Britain and one or more other religious traditions.

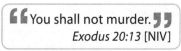

TIP
Make sure you choose contrasting viewpoints.

(B) **Develop** the following argument to support the statement, 'There are no good reasons for countries to possess nuclear weapons' by referring to a relevant religious teaching or quotation.

"Nuclear weapons could kill huge numbers of people and destroy much of the earth. They have a long-lasting impact on the earth because of radiation that will poison the ground. The nuclear winter could last for a very long time, so people would be unable to survive the cold. Food would be scarce and conflict over resources would follow."

6.5 The just war

Essential information:

☐ A **just war** is a war which meets internationally accepted criteria for fairness; follows traditional Christian rules for a just war, and is now accepted by all other religions.

☐ The just war theory gives the conditions that must apply if a war is justifiable and rules on how the war must be fought to make sure it is ethical.

Conditions for a just war

TIP

Try using the mnemonic 'CLIPS' to help you remember some conditions for a just war:

C – just CAUSE
L – LAST resort
I – Right INTENTION
P – PROPORTIONALITY
S – reasonable chance of SUCCESS

But don't forget <u>proper legal authority</u>!

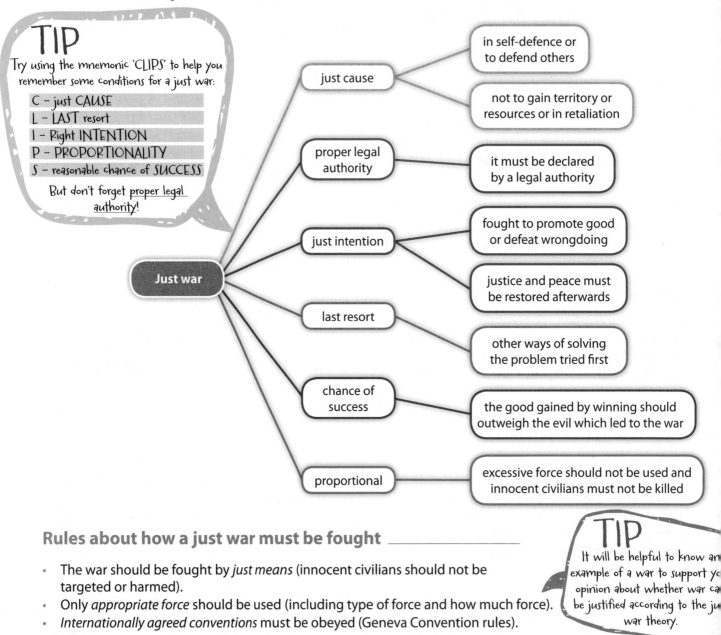

just cause
- in self-defence or to defend others
- not to gain territory or resources or in retaliation

proper legal authority
- it must be declared by a legal authority

just intention
- fought to promote good or defeat wrongdoing
- justice and peace must be restored afterwards

last resort
- other ways of solving the problem tried first

chance of success
- the good gained by winning should outweigh the evil which led to the war

proportional
- excessive force should not be used and innocent civilians must not be killed

Rules about how a just war must be fought

- The war should be fought by *just means* (innocent civilians should not be targeted or harmed).
- Only *appropriate force* should be used (including type of force and how much force).
- *Internationally agreed conventions* must be obeyed (Geneva Convention rules).

TIP

It will be helpful to know an example of a war to support yo opinion about whether war ca be justified according to the ju war theory.

APPLY

A Give **two** conditions of a just war.

B **Develop each of these arguments** for and against the statement, 'The just war theory is the best religious response to whether it is right to fight' by explaining in more detail, adding an example, or referring to a relevant religious teaching or quotation.

For	Against
The just war theory is the best religious response to whether it is right to fight in a war because it is accepted by the United Nations and by all religions. It prevents governments from going to war for selfish reasons, to gain territory or resources, or to get back at an enemy for something they did long ago.	The just war theory is not the best religious response to whether it is right to fight because it accepts that war is sometimes right, when it is never right. The best religious response is to say that war is always wrong.

6.6 Holy war and religion as a cause of violence

Essential information:

- [ ] A **holy war** is fighting for a religious cause or God, probably controlled by a religious leader.
- [ ] Religion is sometimes seen as a cause of violence in the contemporary world.
- [ ] For most Christians the teachings of Jesus make it clear that the use of violence is not justified.

What is a holy war?

- A holy war seems to be a contradiction – how can killing large numbers of people be holy?
- The Old Testament has references to God helping the Jews win battles to settle in the Promised Land.
- In the Crusades (11th to 14th century battles between Christians and Muslims) both sides believed God was on their side.
- For Christians a holy war must:
  - be authorised by a religious leader with great authority
  - only be fought to defend the Christian faith from attack.
- Those who take part gain spiritual rewards (e.g. if they die in battle they will go straight to heaven).
- Christians today stand up for their faith through the power of argument rather than through military strength.

Religion as a cause of violence in the UK

- In the UK today most Christians do not respond violently to an attack on their faith.
- Some denominations of Christianity, particularly Catholics and Protestants, have clashed in the past.
- During 'the Troubles' in Northern Ireland (1968–98) conflict between Catholics and Protestants led to acts of discrimination and violence against each community.
- Although some conflicts may seem to be about two religious groups fighting each other, the reasons for conflict may be more political or economic than religious.

TIP
Do NOT use the conflict in Northern Ireland as an example of a holy war.

Christian beliefs about war and violence

- Some Christians use 'eye for eye, tooth for tooth' (Exodus 21:24) to justify retaliation, but this teaching was intended to reduce violence by limiting retaliation to the individual offenders rather than their whole tribe, many of whom were innocent.
- Most Christians accept Jesus' teaching that not only violence, but the anger that leads to violence, is wrong.

> ❝ You have heard that it was said… "You shall not murder…" but I tell you that anyone who is angry with a brother or sister will be subject to judgement. ❞
> *Matthew 5:21–22 [NIV]*

- Some Christians say Jesus advised his disciples to buy a sword (Luke 22:36) as justification for violence, but most believe Jesus was merely warning his disciples of dangerous times ahead and not suggesting they should take up arms.
- Jesus' example at his arrest showed his non-violent stance:

> ❝ "Put your sword back in its place," Jesus said, "for all who draw the sword die by the sword". ❞
> *Matthew 26:52 [NIV]*

A Give **two** features of holy wars.

B **Evaluate the statement**, 'There is no place for a holy war in contemporary Britain.'

RECAP

Essential information:

☐ **Pacifism** is the belief of people who refuse to take part in war and any other form of violence.

☐ A **peacemaker** is someone who works to establish peace in the world or in a certain part of it.

☐ **Peacemaking** is the action of trying to establish peace.

What is pacifism?

- Pacifists believe that:
  - war and violence can rarely be justified
  - conflicts can be settled in a peaceful way
  - preventing war through promoting justice and peace is a better way
  - prayer and meditation can help people be at peace with themselves and others.
- Christian pacifists follow Jesus' example and teaching:

> ❝ Blessed are the peacemakers, for they shall be called children of God. ❞
> *Matthew 5:9* [NIV]

> You might be asked to compare beliefs on pacifism between Christianity (the main religious tradition in Great Britain) and another religious tradition.

- The Religious Society of Friends (Quakers) are a Christian denomination that strongly supports pacifism.
- During the First and Second World Wars some people called conscientious objectors refused to fight and faced punishment.
- Many conscientious objectors took non-fighting roles as cooks, doctors, nurses or mechanics instead, e.g. volunteering for the Friends' Ambulance Unit.

Modern peacemakers

The Anglican Pacifist Fellowship

- Believe Jesus' teaching is incompatible with the waging of war.
- Believe that the Christian Church should never support or justify war.
- Argue that Christian witness should include opposing the waging or justifying of war.

The Peace People

- Founded in 1976 in Northern Ireland by Mairead Corrigan with Betty Williams and Ciaran McKeown.
- Mairead, a Catholic, and Betty, a Protestant, won the 1976 Nobel Peace Prize for organising marches and events that brought the two communities together.
- The marches showed that many Catholics and Protestants were united in wanting peace rather than the violence and killings taking place at the time.

> ❝ We believe that as Christians we are called to follow the way of Jesus in loving our enemies and becoming peacemakers. ❞ *The Anglican Pacifist Fellowship*

> **TIP**
> Not all Christians are pacifists. Many believe war is right in certain circumstances.

APPLY

A Here are **two** contrasting beliefs in contemporary British society about pacifism. Develop both points by explaining in more detail, adding an example, or referring to a relevant religious teaching or quotation.

First contrasting belief	Second contrasting belief
Some Christians are pacifists who refuse to take part in war or violence of any kind.	Other Christians support peace but are not pacifists.

B Write down **two** reasons in support of the statement, 'Promoting justice and human rights is the best way of preventing conflict'. Now develop each reason by explaining in more detail or by giving examples.

6.8 Christian responses to victims of war

Essential information:

☐ Victims of war include:
   - injured members of the armed forces
   - the families of those who died or were injured in war
   - civilians left in a war zone where everything has been destroyed
   - refugees from war-torn countries.

☐ In Britain the state provides financial and medical help for members of the armed forces and their families affected by war.

☐ Christians believe they should support victims of war to show love of neighbour.

☐ Christian charities such as Caritas and Christian Aid provide help.

Providing help to victims of war

Christians support organisations that help victims because:

- Jesus taught 'Love your neighbour as yourself' (Mark 12:31 [NIV]).
- Jesus' parable of the Good Samaritan (Luke 10:25–37) taught that everyone is everybody else's neighbour, regardless of race, age, gender, religion or political beliefs.
- **Caritas** is a Catholic organisation that serves the poor and promotes charity and justice worldwide. In 2015 it provided food, shelter, translators and legal services to Syrian refugees who had made the dangerous journey to Greece.
- **Christian Aid** (see page 41) is an organisation that tries to end poverty, including poverty caused by war. It tries to prevent war by establishing basic human rights and fairness in societies, as well as supporting local organisations that help refugees from places like Gaza, Afghanistan and Syria.

Victims may need:
- money to live if the main wage earner died
- psychological support
- medical help for injuries
- means of working to earn a living
- a safe place to live
- access to food and clean water

TIP

Be careful to choose a <u>religious</u> organisation that helps victims of war, rather than secular charities like Help for Heroes or the Red Cross which do good work but which are not required for this examination.

Christian Aid (see page 41)

APPLY

A Give **two** ways in which religious believers help victims of war.

B Use the table below to explain why you agree or disagree with the statement, 'The point of war is to kill the enemy, not help them to survive.'

For	Against
If a country has taken the serious decision to go to war, it should try to defeat the enemy as quickly as possible so that the war is ended.	According to the conditions of a just war, only appropriate force should be used, so if the enemy tries to surrender, they should not be killed.
This would prevent more loss of life, for example innocent civilians being killed in a long, drawn-out conflict.	Innocent civilians on the enemy side must be protected and helped to survive.
The enemy is likely to want to kill the soldiers fighting the war, so it is morally right to kill them first.	Paul teaches, 'Do not repay anyone evil for evil… If it is possible, as far as it depends on you, live at peace with everyone.'
Often in war it is impractical to take the enemy prisoner to help them to survive.	This means that even though a just war is being fought, treatment of the enemy should be as compassionate as possible under the circumstances.

Test the 1 mark question

1 Which **one** of the following best expresses the religious ideal of bringing about what is right and fair?

A Peace   B Forgiveness   C Justice   D Defence   **[1 mark]**

2 Which **one** of the following are **not** weapons of mass destruction?

A Chemical weapons   B Nuclear weapons   C Biological weapons   D Conventional weapons   **[1 mark]**

Test the 2 mark question

3 Give **two** conditions of a just war.   **[2 marks]**

1) _____

2) _____

4 Give **two** reasons why many religious people do **not** support violent protest.   **[2 marks]**

1) _____

2) _____

Test the 4 mark question

5 Explain **two** contrasting beliefs in contemporary British society about whether countries should possess weapons of mass destruction. In your answer you should refer to the main religious tradition of Great Britain and one or more other religious traditions.   **[4 marks]**

● **Explain one belief.**	Many Christians, while following Jesus' teaching to 'turn the other cheek' and not to use violence, might approve of countries possessing some weapons of mass destruction in order to stop people being tempted to use them.
● Develop your explanation with more detail/an example/ reference to a religious teaching or quotation.	They would believe that possessing them is necessary in order to prevent war and help to keep the peace.
● **Explain a second contrasting belief.**	No religion agrees with the use of weapons of mass destruction, but some Christians would also disagree with countries possessing them. Quakers are pacifists, opposed to using violence in any circumstances, so they would say that possessing these powerful weapons might encourage a country to use them.
● Develop your explanation with more detail/an example/ reference to a religious teaching or quotation.	This would go against the commandment 'You shall not murder' and against Jesus' teaching to 'love your neighbour'.

TIP
Read the question carefully. It asks for beliefs about whether countries should 'possess' weapons of mass destruction, not whether they should 'use' them.

6 Explain **two** contrasting beliefs in contemporary British society about pacifism. In your answer you should refer to the main religious tradition of Great Britain and one or more other religious traditions.   **[4 marks]**

● **Explain one belief.**	
● Develop your explanation with more detail/an example/ reference to a religious teaching or quotation.	
● **Explain a second contrasting belief.**	
● Develop your explanation with more detail/an example/ reference to a religious teaching or quotation.	

6 Exam practice

7 Explain **two** similar religious beliefs about forgiveness.

In your answer you must refer to one or more religious traditions. **[4 marks]**

Test the 5 mark question

8 Explain **two** religious beliefs about helping victims of war.

Refer to sacred writings or another source of religious belief and teaching in your answer. **[5 marks]**

● **Explain one belief.**	*One Christian belief about helping victims of war is that Christians should treat everyone as if they were a neighbour to them.*
● Develop your explanation with more detail/an example.	*Victims of war may be suffering because they have lost everything, including people they love, so even if Christians do not know them, they should not ignore their suffering but offer to help them in whatever way they can.*
● **Explain a second belief.**	*Christians also believe Jesus taught his followers that to care for those most in need was also to care for him.*
● Develop your explanation with more detail/an example.	*So when a Christian offers help to someone in a desperate situation, they believe they are getting closer to God.*
● Add a reference to sacred writings or another source of religious belief and teaching. If you prefer, you can add this reference to your first belief instead.	*In the parable of the Sheep and the Goats, Jesus says 'Truly I tell you, whatever you did for one of the least of these brothers and sisters of mine, you did for me.' (Matthew 25:40)*

TIP

This answer is particularly good because it includes Christian teaching in both parts of the answer. 'Love your neighbour' is implied in the first sentence even though it is not quoted exactly. If you cannot remember an exact quotation, try to sum up its meaning to support your answer.

9 Explain **two** reasons why some religious people believe it is right to fight in a war.

Refer to sacred writings or another source of religious belief and teaching in your answer. **[5 marks]**

● **Explain one reason.**	
● Develop your explanation with more detail/an example.	
● **Explain a second reason.**	
● Develop your explanation with more detail/an example.	
● Add a reference to sacred writings or another source of religious belief and teaching. If you prefer, you can add this reference to your first belief instead.	

10 Explain **two** religious beliefs about reconciliation.

Refer to sacred writings or another source of religious belief and teaching in your answer. **[5 marks]**

Test the 12 mark question

11 'The just war theory is the best religious response to whether it is right to fight.'

Evaluate this statement. In your answer you:

- should give reasoned arguments in support of this statement
- should give reasoned arguments to support a different point of view
- should refer to religious arguments
- may refer to non-religious arguments
- should reach a justified conclusion.

[12 mark
Plus SPaG 3 ma

REASONED ARGUMENTS IN SUPPORT OF THE STATEMENT ● **Explain why some people would agree with the statement.** ● Develop your explanation with more detail and examples. ● Refer to religious teaching. Use a quote or paraphrase or refer to a religious authority. ● **Evaluate the arguments.** Is this a good argument or not? Explain why you think this.	*Although religious people think it is better to avoid war and violence, if faced with a decision about whether or not it is right to fight, the just war theory gives them some guidance. The theory has several criteria including that the war must be declared by a leader of a state, it should be proportional in the amount of force that is used and that civilians should be protected.* *The theory is a good response because it makes sure wars are not fought about something unimportant or in a way which breaks internationally agreed rules. This is important because God wants people to protect innocent people rather than killing them. The just war theory was invented by a Christian called Augustine and developed by Thomas Aquinas so that is why Christians follow it. Also the Bible teaches 'You shall not murder'. If wars are not just wars, more people will die, and they may be fighting for a wrong reason.*
REASONED ARGUMENTS SUPPORTING A DIFFERENT VIEW ● **Explain why some people would support a different view.** ● Develop your explanation with more detail and examples. ● Refer to religious teaching. Use a quote or paraphrase or refer to a religious authority. ● **Evaluate the arguments.** Is this a good argument or not? Explain why you think this.	*Some Christians do not agree with the just war theory. These Christians may be pacifists like the Quakers who think that all war is wrong whether it is considered 'just' or not. The best religious response to whether it is right to fight is to follow the teaching of Jesus, who said 'Blessed are the peacemakers'. Jesus taught people to 'turn the other cheek' and he forgave his persecutors on the cross.*
CONCLUSION ● **Give a justified conclusion.** ● Include your own opinion together with your own reasoning. ● **Include evaluation.** Explain why you think one viewpoint is stronger than the other or why they are equally strong. ● Do not just repeat arguments you have already used without explaining how they apply to your reasoned opinion/conclusion.	*In conclusion, I would agree with the statement that the just war theory is the right religious response. I have sympathy with the views of pacifists, and ideally war should be avoided, but in the real world there are always countries that will bully other countries or try to take their land or resources, so war is sometimes necessary. It is better to have rules that limit the damage war can do, and the just war theory helps in that way.*

TIP
The first paragraph shows an excellent chain of reasoning. It starts by giving strong support to the statement and then demonstrates detaile knowledge of what the ju war theory says. In the sec paragraph it goes back to issue of whether it is a good religious respons and includes Christiar teaching.

TIP
This is a good example of a justified conclusion as the student gives reasons for their opinion.

12   'Religion is the main cause of wars.'

Evaluate this statement. In your answer you:

- should give reasoned arguments in support of this statement
- should give reasoned arguments to support a different point of view
- should refer to religious arguments
- may refer to non-religious arguments
- should reach a justified conclusion.

[12 marks]
Plus SPaG 3 marks

REASONED ARGUMENTS IN SUPPORT OF THE STATEMENT ● **Explain why some people would agree with the statement.** ● Develop your explanation with more detail and examples. ● Refer to religious teaching. Use a quote or paraphrase or refer to a religious authority. ● **Evaluate the arguments.** Is this a good argument or not? Explain why you think this.	**TIP** When evaluation questions ask whether something is the 'main' cause or 'best' response or whether a religious belief is the 'most important' belief, they are asking you to think about whether other causes/responses/beliefs are more significant or whether there can be many of equal merit.
REASONED ARGUMENTS SUPPORTING A DIFFERENT VIEW ● **Explain why some people would support a different view.** ● Develop your explanation with more detail and examples. ● Refer to religious teaching. Use a quote or paraphrase or refer to a religious authority. ● **Evaluate the arguments.** Is this a good argument or not? Explain why you think this.	
CONCLUSION ● **Give a justified conclusion.** ● Include your own opinion together with your own reasoning. ● **Include evaluation.** Explain why you think one viewpoint is stronger than the other or why they are equally strong. ● Do not just repeat arguments you have already used without explaining how they apply to your reasoned opinion/conclusion.	

13   'Religious people should be the main peacemakers in the world today.'

Evaluate this statement. In your answer you:

- should give reasoned arguments in support of this statement
- should give reasoned arguments to support a different point of view
- should refer to religious arguments
- may refer to non-religious arguments
- should reach a justified conclusion.

[12 marks]
Plus SPaG 3 marks

Check your answers using the mark scheme on page 125. How did you do?
To feel more secure in the content you need to remember, re-read pages 82–89.
To remind yourself of what the examiner is looking for, go to pages 6–11.

7.1 Crime and punishment

Essential information:

☐ A **crime** is an offence that is punishable by law.

☐ **Punishment** is something legally done to someone who has been found guilty of breaking the law.

Crime and punishment

- People who commit crimes face legal consequences.
- If the police suspect someone of committing a crime and there is evidence to support this, that person can be arrested. They are then questioned and if the police are confident they have the right person, they are charged.
- In the UK, magistrates and, for more serious cases, crown courts are involved in hearing cases against someone charged with committing a crime.
- The courts decide whether the accused is *guilty* or *not guilty* and if guilty, impose a sentence as punishment.
- In the UK, the most severe sentence is life in prison. There is no death penalty.

Good and evil intentions and actions

Some people assume a **good action** is an action that does not break a law. However, there are many good actions that people perform that exist outside the law.

- There is no law telling people that they have to give to charity or to help people in need.
- Being kind and compassionate is a natural human reaction and has nothing to do with the law.
- People who do such good things intend to do them; it is not accidental.
- However, some Christians believe that legal actions such as adultery and abortion are wrong despite them not being illegal.
- Actions encouraged by genuine religious faith are good.

There are many **evil actions** that are against the law.

- Evil actions may cause suffering, injury or death.
- Christians usually use the word evil to refer to actions that are profoundly immoral and wicked and are against God.
- Not all evil actions come from evil intentions; sometimes a person may be influenced by the situation which they find themselves in and end up doing something wicked without setting out to.

Christian responses to good and evil intentions and actions

Christians recognise that:

- no person is evil
- humans are not perfect and make mistakes
- the original sin of Adam and Eve gives some humans a tendency to do wicked things on occasions
- because people are created good, there is usually a reason why humans do wicked things
- this reason could be a psychological illness that should be treated in addition to the person being punished for their wicked actions.

APPLY

(A) Explain **two** Christian responses to good and evil intentions and actions.

(B) 'Intentions are more important than actions.'

Write a developed argument on each side of this statement. Elaborate your arguments with religious teaching.

TIP

When faced with a statement that you strongly agree or disagree with, you must also focus on an alternative opinion, even if you cannot understand why anybody should believe it.

Essential information:

☐ Christians believe crime is hardly ever justified, no matter what the reason for it is.

☐ Some reasons why people might commit crimes are **poverty** (being without money, food or other basic needs), **mental illness** (a condition that affects a person's emotions or moods), **addiction** (a physical or mental dependency on a substance or activity which is very difficult to overcome) and **greed** (wanting to possess wealth or items that are not needed).

Reasons why some people commit crime

Christians believe that laws are important for keeping order in society so that people may live in peace.

> ❝ Let everyone be subject to the governing authorities, for there is no authority except that which God has established. ❞
>
> *Romans 13:1 [NIV]*

Christians believe that, whatever the reason for committing a crime may be, there is hardly ever any justification for doing so. However, they do believe that Christians should help prevent people committing crimes. So while they condemn stealing, they are keen to make sure that nobody is so poor that they use poverty as a reason for stealing.

> ❝ Focusing on poverty and sacrificing for the poor are the heart of the gospel. If Christians don't dig deep and generously open up their wallets, they do not have genuine faith. ❞
>
> *Pope Francis*

Reason	More detail	Christian view
Poverty	There are millions of people in the UK who live in poverty and cannot always afford to buy food, so some steal food for their family.	Society should ensure that no one finds themselves in the position of having to steal food. Christians support food banks and may campaign for the living wage and to improve public services.
Upbringing	Some people grow up in a household where crime is a way of life and they may be encouraged by their parents to commit crime.	Parents should teach their children the right way to behave through their own words and actions.
Mental illness	Some forms of mental illness may lead people into crime. Anger management problems and depression may lead to violence and drug abuse.	Christians believe that treating the causes of the illness is the most loving and compassionate way of dealing with people with mental illness.
Addiction	Taking illegal drugs is a crime, even though the person is addicted. They may commit further crimes to be able to buy drugs. Legal drugs, e.g. alcohol, can also play a part in crimes such as violence, rape and drunk driving.	Christians are against taking illegal drugs and support rehabilitation as a way of defeating the addiction. Christians permit alcohol but not to excess.
Greed	Some people want personal possessions that they do not need and cannot afford. Their greed for them may lead them to steal.	The Ten Commandments forbid envy and it is envy that often causes greed.
Hate	Hate, the opposite of love, can lead to violence or aggression.	Jesus taught to love everybody, including your enemies.
Opposition to an unjust law	Some people break laws that they believe to be unjust in order to protest against them.	Some Christians may agree with this but only if no violence is involved and nobody gets harmed.

Obeying the law helps society to live in peace without fear of danger. Regardless of the reasons why crimes are committed, most crimes are selfish because they harm innocent people so that the criminal can get what they want or need.

Ⓐ Explain **two** reasons why people commit crimes.

Ⓑ 'Addiction is the only good reason for committing crimes.'

Write down your own thoughts about this and **develop them by adding religious views**.

> TIP
>
> If you want to include a personal example you know about in your answer, you may want to change the person's name.

7.3 Christian attitudes to lawbreakers and different types of crime

Essential information:

☐ Many Christians have compassionate attitudes to lawbreakers but condemn the crimes they commit.

Christian attitudes to lawbreakers

Christians believe the law should be respected and they generally support the UK legal system.

- The law states that a person is innocent until the court proves that they are guilty.
- If any doubt exists, the person is innocent and allowed to continue with their life normally and without punishment.
- Everyone is treated equally under the law.
- In trials heard by a jury, fellow citizens make the decision on guilt (but not the punishment).
- Once a person is found guilty, the judge, using legal guidelines, decides on a punishment.

Many Christians hate the crime but not the criminal who committed it. They believe that:

- offenders must be punished by the law according to how serious the crime was
- offenders have basic rights and so should not be given a punishment that is harmful
- through their punishment offenders should be helped to become useful members of society so they do not reoffend
- the parable of the Sheep and the Goats makes it clear that helping prisoners is good.

Some Christians prefer the punishment to be as severe as the crime committed, including the death penalty for those who intentionally kill another person.

> **TIP**
> Just because Christians favour punishments that are helpful to the criminal and not harmful, it does not mean they think punishment is wrong.

> 66 Come, you who are blessed by my Father; take your inheritance, the kingdom prepared for you since the creation of the world. For… I was in prison and you came to visit me. 99
> *Matthew 25:34–36* [NIV]

Different types of crime – hate crime, theft and murder

Hate crimes often involve violence and are usually targeted at a person because of their race, religion, sexuality, disability or gender.

Theft is less serious than some other crimes but it still results in a victim suffering a loss.

Murder is one of the worst crimes. Some murders involve the victim being submitted to great pain before they die. Some murders are classed as hate crimes.

Christian attitudes to different types of crime

Christians believe that crime is wrong.

- When Jesus taught people to love their neighbour, he expected them to show compassion, care and respect for everyone. This means that Jesus himself would condemn criminal actions because no crime shows love towards the victim.
- Both murder and theft are not permitted in the Ten Commandments.

> 66 You shall not murder. 99   *Exodus 20:13* [NIV]

> 66 You shall not steal. 99   *Exodus 20:15* [NIV]

- Christians do not justify theft caused by the need to supply food to a family. They will look for an alternative way to provide food such as through a food bank, helping people to find a job or campaigning for a fairer society.

A   Explain the similarities and differences between a hate crime and murder.

B   Should Christians hate the crime but not the criminal who has committed it?

Explain your opinion and elaborate it with religious teachings.

> **TIP**
> When elaborating a developed idea with religious teachings, you should show how the teachings are relevant.

RECAP

Essential information:

☐ The three aims of punishment are retribution, deterrence and reformation.

Aims	More detail	What do Christians believe?
Retribution – to get your own back	• Society is getting its own back on the offender. • It is supported by the Old Testament idea of 'life for life, eye for eye, tooth for tooth…' (Exodus 21:23–24 [NIV]) which is interpreted as meaning that criminals should receive back the same (not greater) injuries and harm that their criminal actions caused. • In the case of murder, the murderer should be killed as a punishment.	• Christians believe the 'eye for eye' teaching should not be taken literally but that punishment should be severe enough (but not more severe) to match the seriousness of the crime. • This means murderers should not necessarily be killed as punishment. • Most Christians prefer other aims which they believe are less harmful and more positive.
Deterrence – to put people off committing crimes	• The idea of deterrence is to use the punishment an offender receives as an example and warning to others considering a similar crime. • If the punishment is harsh, it is less likely that others are going to copy the offender. • In addition, harsh punishment may deter the offender from repeating their crime. • In some countries, and many years ago in the UK, punishments were carried out in public to make sure people saw for themselves what happens to offenders.	• Although most Christians have no real problem with deterring people from committing crimes, they do not support punishments that are so excessively harsh that they cause physical or mental harm to the offender or infringe their rights. • They oppose carrying out punishments in public because they could humiliate offenders rather than treating them with respect, despite what they have done.
Reformation – to change someone's behaviour for the better	• Reformation tries to help offenders while punishing them. • They may be given group therapy sessions, individual counselling and made to carry out community service to help them to understand that their behaviour was wrong because it harmed society. • It is hoped that offenders will be taught to change their attitude so that they can take their place back in the community as a responsible law-abiding citizen.	• Most Christians favour reformation over other aims of punishment. • It is positive rather than negative and works with individuals to improve their life chances by turning their life around. • It is not a replacement for punishment but happens alongside punishment even for the worst offenders who are kept in prison.

Paul summed up the Christian response to punishment in his letter to the Romans:

> ❝ Do not take revenge, my dear friends… On the contrary:… Do not be overcome by evil, but overcome evil with good. ❞ *Romans 12:19–21 [NIV]*

TIP
To protect other people in the community is another aim of punishment that you can use if you wish.

APPLY

A Write **two** sentences to explain what each of the three aims of punishment are.

B **Write a detailed argument** to support your own opinion about whether offenders should be punished severely. Try to include some Christian teaching.

TIP
The three aims of punishment may be useful to develop your ideas if writing about other aspects of punishment.

7.5 Christian attitudes to suffering and causing suffering to others

Essential information:

☐ Christians believe they should help those who are suffering.

☐ Christians believe that they must not ignore causing suffering to others.

Christian attitudes to suffering

Suffering is an unfortunate part of life that no one can avoid. It can be:

- caused by a natural event such as a storm, drought or earthquake
- caused by an illness
- self-inflicted, such as crashing a car into a tree or self-harming
- caused by the behaviour of someone else such as assault, burglary or passive smoking.

Whatever the cause, Christians believe they have a duty to help those who are suffering and recognise that good can come from suffering. Paul, who suffered greatly at some points in his life wrote:

> ❝We also glory in our sufferings, because we know that suffering produces perseverance; perseverance, character; and character, hope. ❞   *Romans 5:3–4 [NIV]*

Christians try to follow the example of Jesus. He helped many whom he saw were suffering and told his followers to do the same.

Why does a loving God allow people to suffer?

- It is wrong to blame God for suffering resulting from what are usually human actions.
- God could control people to stop them from doing wrong. Instead, Christians believe that he gave humans **free will**, the ability to make decisions for themselves.
- This does not mean that humans can do whatever they want, whenever they want to do it. This would certainly not prevent suffering. If anything, it would increase it.

TIP

It is very important that you understand these points, so make sure you study them carefully.

According to Christians, God has given plenty of guidance about how to use free will responsibly. The teachings and example of Jesus, if followed, would reduce suffering. The role of the law is to give more 'compulsory guidance' about the best way to use free will, together with punishments for those who cause suffering by committing crimes.

Christian attitudes to causing suffering to others

- Christians are generally opposed to causing others to suffer.
- Jesus taught that people should love and respect each other and not even use violence in self-defence because it may increase suffering, not reduce it.
- However, this does not always work and on occasions, maybe accidentally, Christians do cause others to suffer.
- If and when that happens, Christians are taught to apologise and to try to repair the damage they have caused in order to restore relationships afterwards.
- Jesus gave an example of this at his arrest. One of the disciples reacted to Jesus being arrested by cutting off the High Priest's servant's ear. Jesus rebuked the disciple and then healed the servant.
- Christians try to heal the wrong that has been done and the suffering that has been caused in whatever way they can. This is the message Jesus gave.

APPLY

(A) Explain carefully what Christians believe about free will and how it should be used.

(B) 'Using violence in self-defence only causes more suffering.'

Think carefully about this and **write a developed argument** to support your opinion about it.

7.6 Christian attitudes to the treatment of criminals – prison, corporal punishment and community service

Essential information:

☐ The three forms of punishment are **prison** (a secure building where offenders are held for a period of time), **corporal punishment** (punishment causing physical pain) and **community service** (unpaid work in the community).

☐ Christian beliefs and attitudes to the treatment of criminals are compassionate.

> You might be asked to compare beliefs on corporal punishment between Christianity (the main religious tradition in Great Britain) and another religious tradition.

Punishment	Features	Religious views
Prison	• Punishment is loss of liberty • For serious crimes • No real choice about how to spend their time – everything is controlled for them • Locked in cells, fed and allowed exercise and interaction with other prisoners at set times • Prisoners work in the prison for very little money or take part in training or education programmes	Many Christians believe that prisoners should be treated well when in prison and are keen to support them to make their time in prison useful by encouraging positive activity. They believe it is important that conditions within prison are humane and civilised.
Corporal punishment	• Punishes offenders by inflicting physical pain • Illegal in the UK and many other countries • Punishments often take place in public • Considered to be a breach of human rights laws	Most Christians do not support corporal punishment. It does not seek to reform an offender, so can be seen as a negative and harmful punishment.
Community service	• Includes work in the community, such as cleaning graffiti off buildings or clearing wasteland • Considered to be a punishment for minor offences, such as vandalism or benefit fraud • Gives offenders the chance to make up for what they have done and reform • It can include treatment for addiction or medical conditions, counselling or educational opportunities	Christians agree with community service for offenders who they think may benefit. It allows them to make up for what they have done wrong (reparation), deters them from committing offences in the future and reforms them by making them realise the consequences of their actions. No harm is done to the offender and it is hoped that the experience is positive.

APPLY

A Give **two** reasons why most Christians do not support corporal punishment.

B 'Criminals should not be treated well.'

What religious arguments would you include when evaluating this statement?

RECAP

Essential information:

☐ Following the teaching and example of Jesus, Christians believe that forgiveness is an important concept.

> **TIP**
> It is very important to be clear that no religions consider forgiveness to be a replacement for the legal process of punishing offenders. In the UK, a person convicted of murder will receive a lengthy prison sentence regardless of whether friends and family of the victim have forgiven them.

Forgiveness

- **Forgiveness** literally means to show mercy and pardon someone for what they have done wrong.
- It is a key belief in Christianity and one that Jesus showed in his actions and taught to his followers.
- However, it exists outside the legal system of crime and punishment, so has no effect on deciding whether someone is innocent or guilty, nor on sentencing.
- When he was being crucified, Jesus forgave those who crucified him after having been found guilty and sentenced to death:

> **"** Father forgive them, for they do not know what they are doing. **"**   *Luke 23:34* [NIV]

- Christians believe that **God expects them to show forgiveness** to others, no matter what they may have done. In turn, they believe that **God will forgive them for any sins they may commit.** This is emphasised in the Lord's Prayer:

> **"** Forgive us our sins as we forgive those who sin against us. **"**   *The Lord's Prayer*

> **TIP**
> See page 82 to read about forgiveness in the context of war.

- The Christian interpretation of forgiveness related to those who commit crimes is that they should be forgiven as far as possible but that the offender should be punished to ensure that justice is done.
- If the aim of the punishment is to reform, the punishment should benefit the offender.
- Jesus taught his disciples that there was no limit to the number of times that they should forgive someone. (Matthew 18:21–22)

Other faiths' attitudes to forgiveness

Just like Christianity, forgiveness is an important concept in Judaism. However the process of forgiveness is a little different from Christianity.

- The offender needs to show remorse to their victim and honestly ask for their forgiveness.
- The victim has a duty to forgive if they believe the request is genuine.
- Only then can the offender expect to be forgiven by God.
- Forgiveness is an important element in the ten days of repentance between Rosh Hashanah and Yom Kippur, when Jews are encouraged to ask for forgiveness from anyone they have wronged.

Muslim attitudes to forgiveness are also different.

- Only God can truly forgive and will only forgive those he knows are truly sorry and intend to follow the faith properly in the future.
- People should forgive each other in order to allow goodness to be established over evil. The offender should seek the forgiveness of the victim before expecting God to forgive.

> You might be asked to compare beliefs on forgiveness between Christianity (the main religious tradition in Great Britain) and another religious tradition.

APPLY

(A) Explain **two** contrasting beliefs about forgiveness.

(B) 'Nobody should expect to be forgiven more than once.'

   Write a logical chain of reasoning (include an opinion, a reason, development and elaboration through adding religious teaching) that agrees with this statement and one that gives a different point of view.

Essential information:

☐ The **death penalty** is a form of punishment in which the prisoner is put to death for crimes committed.

☐ Arguments about the death penalty are often based on the principle of utility and the sanctity of life.

Arguments concerning the death penalty

Innocent people may die:

- Innocent people who were incorrectly found guilty of serious crimes have been executed in error. The chance of killing an innocent person is one of the arguments against the death penalty.
- Three people executed in the UK in the 1950s have since been pardoned because new evidence has cast serious doubt over their guilt.
- Since its abolition in 1969, several people who would have faced the death penalty, had it been allowed, were freed from prison because they were innocent.

The principle of utility:

- The principle of utility states that an action is right if it produces the maximum happiness for the greatest number of people affected by it.
- If the use of the death penalty is proven to protect society it can be justified.
- However, if it is done to show retribution, it is wrong.

The sanctity of life:

- The **sanctity of life** is the teaching that all life is holy as it is created by God, and only God can take it away.
- However, some believe that, as offenders have already taken life, God approves of them being punished in a way they deserve.
- The Old Testament, using the teaching 'eye for eye' (Exodus 21:24 [NIV]) can be used to support this view.

Christian attitudes to the death penalty

Christians across many denominations have different views about the death penalty. Some of the arguments they use are based on Bible passages and others relate to general Christian and social principles.

> You might be asked to compare beliefs on the death penalty between Christianity (the main religious tradition in Great Britain) and another religious tradition.

Agree	Disagree
• Genesis 9:6 and Exodus 21:23–24 teach retribution. • The death penalty is justified retribution for people who commit the worst possible crimes. • It deters people from committing horrific crimes because they know what will happen to them. • It protects society by removing the worst criminals so they cannot cause harm again.	• God gave life and only God has the right and authority to take it. • Ezekiel 33:11 teaches that wrongdoers should be reformed. • The best aim of punishment is reformation. A dead criminal cannot be reformed. • There is little evidence that the death penalty is a deterrent; the UK murder rate is no higher than in countries that have the death penalty. • Many murders are not planned. The threat of punishment doesn't enter into the murderer's thinking.

Ⓐ Give **two** Christian teachings about the death penalty.

Ⓑ **Write a paragraph** to support the statement, 'Christians should not support the death penalty.'

Test the 1 mark question

1. Which **one** of the following punishments is illegal in the UK?

   A Corporal punihment   B Prison   C Paying a fine   D Community service   **[1 mark]**

2. Which **one** of the following reflects the principle of utility, which suggests an action is right if it promotes maximum…?

   A Pain   B Sadness   C Happiness   D Profit   **[1 mark]**

Test the 2 mark question

3. Give **two** aims of punishment.   **[2 marks]**

   1) _____

   2) _____

4. Give **two** different reasons why some people commit crimes.   **[2 marks]**

   1) _____

   2) _____

Test the 4 mark question

5. Explain **two** contrasting beliefs in contemporary British society about whether the death penalty should exist in the UK.

   In your answer you should refer to the main religious tradition of Great Britain and one or more other religious traditions.   **[4 ma**

● **Explain one belief.**	*Some Christians believe that the death penalty is correct because it follows the Old Testament teaching of 'eye for eye, tooth for tooth'.*
● Develop your explanation with more detail/an example/reference to a religious teaching or quotation.	*'Eye for eye, tooth for tooth' means that an offender should receive back the same as he has done, so if he has murdered someone, he should be killed.*
● **Explain a second contrasting belief.**	*Buddhists disagree with the death penalty because it goes against the first precept and the eight-fold path.*
● Develop your explanation with more detail/an example/reference to a religious teaching or quotation.	*The first precept forbids Buddhists from harming or killing any living being as it goes against right action in the eight-fold path.*

TIP

Both of the explanations of beliefs in this answer have been clearly developed with religious teaching.

6. Explain **two** contrasting beliefs about community service.   **[4 marks]**

● **Explain one belief.**	
● Develop your explanation with more detail/an example/reference to a religious teaching or quotation.	
● **Explain a second contrasting belief.**	
● Develop your explanation with more detail/an example/reference to a religious teaching or quotation.	

7 Exam practice

7 Explain **two** similar beliefs that support retribution as an aim of punishment.

In your answer you should refer to the main religious tradition of Great Britain and one or more other religious traditions. **[4 marks]**

Test the 5 mark question

8 Explain **two** religious beliefs about reformation as an aim of punishment.

Refer to sacred writings or another source of religious belief and teaching in your answer. **[5 marks]**

● **Explain one belief.**	*One Christian belief is that reformation is a preferable aim of punishment because it seeks to help offenders change their behaviour.*
● Develop your explanation with more detail/an example.	*This means they are less likely to commit any further offences, so they won't hurt anybody else or need to be punished again.*
● **Describe a second belief.**	*A second Christian belief is that reformation is a compassionate response towards wrongdoing.*
● Develop your explanation with more detail/an example.	*Christians believe that to show compassion for others is to follow the teachings of Jesus, who told his disciples to turn the other cheek when evil was done to them.*
● Add a reference to sacred writings or another source of religious belief and teaching. If you prefer, you can add this reference to your first belief instead.	*The words of Paul in Romans 12:21 support this idea: 'do not be overcome by evil, but overcome evil with good.'*

TIP
When using scripture, try to show the examiner that you understand its relevance to the question.

9 Explain **two** religious beliefs about forgiveness.

Refer to sacred writings or another source of religious belief and teaching in your answer. **[5 marks]**

● **Explain one belief.**	
● Develop your explanation with more detail/an example.	
● **Explain a second belief.**	
● Develop your explanation with more detail/an example.	
● Add a reference to sacred writings or another source of religious belief and teaching. If you prefer, you can add this reference to your first belief instead.	

TIP
No religion agrees with hate crimes, they are all against them.

10 Explain **two** religious beliefs about hate crimes.

Refer to sacred writings or another source of religious belief and teaching in your answer. **[5 marks]**

Test the 12 mark question

11 'It is right to forgive all offenders whoever they are and whatever they have done.'

Evaluate this statement. In your answer you:

- should give reasoned arguments in support of this statement
- should give reasoned arguments to support a different point of view
- should refer to religious arguments
- may refer to non-religious arguments
- should reach a justified conclusion.

[12 marks]

Plus SPaG 3 ma

REASONED ARGUMENTS IN SUPPORT OF THE STATEMENT ● **Explain why some people would agree with the statement.** ● Develop your explanation with more detail and examples. ● Refer to religious teaching. Use a quote or paraphrase or refer to a religious authority. ● **Evaluate the arguments.** Is this a good argument or not? Explain why you think this.	*Christians should always forgive anybody who wants to be forgiven. When the disciples asked Jesus how many times they should forgive, suggesting that seven was a fair number, Jesus told them it should be seventy-seven times. In other words, there should be no maximum. Jesus even asked God to forgive the people who crucified him because they didn't know what they were doing. So it should not matter how many times, whoever is asking to be forgiven or what they have done to be forgiven for.* *If someone is forgiven, there is a better chance that they will be reformed and try hard to make sure that whatever they have done is never repeated. This is what repentance is about and forgiveness and repentance are closely linked. No sin is unforgiveable and so people, especially religious people, should always forgive, especially as this does not mean that the sinner is not punished because they have been forgiven.*
REASONED ARGUMENTS SUPPORTING A DIFFERENT VIEW ● **Explain why some people would support a different view.** ● Develop your explanation with more detail and examples. ● Refer to religious teaching. Use a quote or paraphrase or refer to a religious authority. ● **Evaluate the arguments.** Is this a good argument or not? Explain why you think this.	*Some people who are victims of serious crimes find it very difficult to forgive. They cannot imagine how they can ever feel anything but hatred for someone who has wronged them so horribly. A victim of rape may find it hard to forgive their attacker and they are highly unlikely to ever forget it. Time is a great healer and maybe forgiveness is more easily given some years later. The line in the Lord's Prayer that says: 'Forgive us our sins, as we forgive those who sin against us' is unrealistic because there are some awful things that should never be forgiven unless the offender shows they are truly sorry and remorseful, and even then, it is almost impossible. Many Jews find it impossible to forgive the Nazis for the Holocaust and why should they be expected to?*
CONCLUSION ● **Give a justified conclusion.** ● Include your own opinion together with your own reasoning. ● **Include evaluation.** Explain why you think one viewpoint is stronger than the other or why they are equally strong. ● Do not just repeat arguments you have already used without explaining how they apply to your reasoned opinion/conclusion.	*In my opinion, forgiveness is an ideal that religions want people to work towards. I think if they become the victims themselves, they may change their mind. We are only human.*

TIP

The first paragraph not only shows good knowled of the Bible's teaching o forgiveness but also mak its meaning clear. Th next paragraph develo the argument by relati the teaching directly to the statement bei evaluated.

TIP

This student could improve their conclusion by going into more detail about their views on the statement. For example, they could explain why they think one viewpoint is stronger than the other, or express an opinion about the strength of the religious arguments given in the answer.

12 'The idea of the sanctity of life shows the death penalty is wrong.'

Evaluate this statement. In your answer you:

- should give reasoned arguments in support of this statement
- should give reasoned arguments to support a different point of view
- should refer to religious arguments
- may refer to non-religious arguments
- should reach a justified conclusion.

TIP

Don't forget that the focus of the statement is on the <u>sanctity</u> of life and the death penalty, not just whether the death penalty is wrong.

[12 marks]

Plus SPaG 3 marks

REASONED ARGUMENTS IN SUPPORT OF THE STATEMENT ● **Explain why some people would agree with the statement.** ● Develop your explanation with more detail and examples. ● Refer to religious teaching. Use a quote or paraphrase or refer to a religious authority. ● **Evaluate the arguments.** Is this a good argument or not? Explain why you think this.	
REASONED ARGUMENTS SUPPORTING A DIFFERENT VIEW ● **Explain why some people would support a different view.** ● Develop your explanation with more detail and examples. ● Refer to religious teaching. Use a quote or paraphrase or refer to a religious authority. ● **Evaluate the arguments.** Is this a good argument or not? Explain why you think this.	
CONCLUSION ● **Give a justified conclusion.** ● Include your own opinion together with your own reasoning. ● **Include evaluation.** Explain why you think one viewpoint is stronger than the other or why they are equally strong. ● Do not just repeat arguments you have already used without explaining how they apply to your reasoned opinion/conclusion.	

13 'There is no good reason why anyone should commit a crime.'

Evaluate this statement. In your answer you:

- should give reasoned arguments in support of this statement
- should give reasoned arguments to support a different point of view
- should refer to religious arguments
- may refer to non-religious arguments
- should reach a justified conclusion.

[12 marks]

Plus SPaG 3 marks

Check your answers using the mark scheme on page 126. How did you do?

To feel more secure in the content you need to remember, re-read pages 94–101.

To remind yourself of what the examiner is looking for, go to pages 6–11.

8 Religion, human rights and social justice

8.1 Social justice and human rights

Essential information:

☐ **Social justice** means ensuring that society treats people fairly whether they are poor or wealthy and protects people's **human rights**, which are the basic rights and freedoms to which everyone should be entitled.

Human rights

In **1948**, the United Nations adopted the Universal Declaration of Human Rights (UDHR). It sets out the rights that everyone should be entitled to regardless of their nationality, language, religion, gender or status. The UK was a signatory to the UDHR. In **1998**, the UK government passed the Human Rights Act (HRA) that reinforces the UDHR.

The HRA prohibits slavery, torture and forced labour and includes the right to:

- life
- liberty
- security
- privacy
- education
- marriage
- a fair trial
- free elections
- family life

Responsibilities

Having rights gives humans responsibilities to exercise them in such a way that nobody else's rights are infringed.

- Humans have the right to freedom of speech but the responsibility not to say something that causes offence to someone else.
- Children have the right to protection from cruelty, exploitation and neglect but the responsibility not to bully or harm each other.

What do Christians say?

- The Bible teaches that God is a God of justice and it has a lot of teachings about the importance of human justice.
- Some of the Old Testament prophets were quick to condemn those who denied people justice. The prophets looked forward to a fairer society.
- In Romans, Paul told followers:

> **❝** Let justice roll on like a river and righteousness like a never-failing stream. **❞**
> *Amos 5:24 [NIV]*

> **❝** Let everyone be subject to the governing authorities, for there is no authority except that which God has established. **❞**
> *Romans 13:1 [NIV]*

- Jesus stressed the need to help others in his teaching: 'love your neighbour as yourself' (Mark 12:31 [NIV]).
- James reinforced this for the early Christians when he said 'faith without deeds is useless' (James 2:20 [NIV]).

A Choose **two** of the Bible quotes in this section and explain what they tell you about social justice.

B 'Everybody's human rights should be protected.'

Write a detailed argument agreeing with this statement and one for a different opinion.

TIP
If you are including scripture in your answer, don't worry if you can't remember it exactly. It should be fine to paraphrase it, provided you don't change the meaning.

8.2 Prejudice and discrimination

Essential information:

☐ Christians believe in **equality** – that humans are of equal value and status.

☐ **Prejudice** means holding biased opinions about an individual or group without knowing all the facts and **discrimination** is the actions or behaviour that result from prejudice.

Equality

- Christians believe that being created in God's image makes people very special and precious.
- Even though people are born in different parts of the world and in different circumstances, they are equally valuable and can have the same relationship with God.
- Wealth, poverty, religion or gender do not affect this.

> **❝** There is neither Jew nor Gentile, neither slave nor free, nor is there male and female, for you are one in Christ Jesus. **❞**   *Galatians 3:28* [NIV]

Gender prejudice and discrimination

- At the time of the early Christians (first century CE), attitudes to women were very different from nowadays. In Corinthians, Paul wrote:

> **❝** Women should remain silent in the churches… for it is disgraceful for a woman to speak in the church. **❞**   *1 Corinthians 14:34–5* [NIV]

- He also wrote that just as Christ is the head of man, so a man is the head of a woman.
- Many Christians believe that Paul's views and writings are a reflection of the times he lived in. Society has now changed and what 2000 years ago seemed right and normal is not so now.
- In some Christian denominations, women are still unable to hold high positions within the Church.
- The Catholic and Orthodox Churches do not allow women to be priests and it was only in 1993 that women were allowed to hold such a position in the Church of England.
- In 2014, Rev Libby Lane became the first female bishop in the Church of England.
- Muslims allow only men to become imams (leaders of prayer) and Reform (but not Orthodox) Jews allow women to become rabbis in order to lead worship.

> **TIP**
> If you are offering an opinion using Paul's teaching, this point will help you in your evaluation.

> You might be asked to compare beliefs on the status of women in religion between Christianity (the main religious tradition in Great Britain) and another religious tradition.

Sexuality

- Following the teaching in Genesis about Adam and Eve, **heterosexual** relations (between a man and a woman) became considered to be natural and what God intended.
- **Homosexual** relations (between man and man, and woman and woman) were more controversial.
- Christians have mixed views on homosexuality. Some see it as sinful, while others see it as morally acceptable.
- Those who oppose it believe that sexual relations are for creating children, something that homosexual relations cannot do.
- Those who think it acceptable focus more on the love between people.
- Recent changes in UK legislation have given equality to everybody, regardless of sexuality, and homosexual couples can now legally marry.

A Explain the Christian views on prejudice based on sexuality.

B **Write a developed reason** for agreeing that the Church's views are sexist and one for a different opinion.

> **TIP**
> In a question like this, if asked for the Christian position on sexism or any other type of prejudice, it is not necessary for you to include your own opinion.

Essential information:

☐ Christians believe that people have **freedom of religion** (the right to believe whatever religion one chooses), including **religious expression** (the right to practise one's faith in whatever way one chooses).

You might be asked to compare beliefs on freedom of religious expression between Christianity (the main religious tradition in Great Britain) and another religious tradition.

Freedom of religion

- Christianity is the main religious tradition in Great Britain.
- The reigning monarch is the official Head of the Church of England and has been referred to as the 'defender of the faith' since 1521.
- Nobody is forced to be a Christian because the government protects the freedom of religious expression.
- This gives all individuals the right to follow whichever faith they choose or none.
- Laws forbid the persecution of members of any faith and any person can encourage anybody else to follow their faith, provided they do not preach hatred and intolerance.

These freedoms are enshrined in the Universal Declaration of Human Rights:

> ❝Everyone has the right to freedom of thought, conscience and religion; this right includes freedom to change his religion and belief, and freedom… to manifest his religion or belief in teaching, practice, worship and observance. ❞
>
> *UDHR*

- In some parts of the world governments do not allow their citizens such freedoms, for example in Pakistan and the Middle East Christians face persecution. Attacks on churches have cost the lives of many innocent civilians exercising their right to worship.
- Conflict based on politics and a divide between Protestants and Catholics in Northern Ireland during the second half of the twentieth century has largely been ended.

Religious teachings on freedom of religion

Christianity	Islam	Judaism
Christian teaching encourages tolerance and harmony. ❝…be patient, bearing with one another in love.❞ *Ephesians 4:2 [NIV]* Different Christian denominations fighting each other are not following Paul's words: ❝If it is possible… live at peace with everyone.❞ *Romans 12:18 [NIV]*	Muslims believe that religious freedom is part of God's design and freedom of belief is taught in the Qur'an. (Qur'an 18:29) However, Shari'ah law does have provisions to punish people who convert from Islam to another faith, although these are only enforced in a few countries.	Judaism is not a religion that tries to gain followers. Most Jews are born into the faith. Non-Jews (Gentiles) who follow seven basic moral laws given to Noah are regarded as 'righteous among the nations' and are assured of a place in the world to come. The Ten Commandments were originally given to Jews but have now been accepted by people of many faiths and none, as a basis for living a moral life.

A Give a definition for freedom of religion.

B **Explain, with reference to religion,** whether you think people should be free to follow any religion they choose without any interference from anybody else.

TIP
It is important for you to express what you think in the 12 mark questions as well as responding from the point of view of Christianity and or other religions.

Essential information:

☐ Christians oppose racial prejudice and other forms of discrimination.

Racism

Racism means to consider people of different races as inferior and to treat people of these races badly as a result.

- In Britain, racism was made illegal in the 1976 Race Relations Act.
- 'Show Racism the Red Card' is a campaign designed to educate football fans and to remove racist abuse from football.
- Most Christians oppose racism. Paul wrote to the church in Galatia:

> **"** There is neither Jew nor Gentile, neither slave nor free, nor is there male and female for you are one in Christ Jesus. **"**
> *Galatians 3:28* [NIV]

- In twentieth century South Africa, the system of apartheid kept black and white people apart.
- Only white people could vote. Black people did not have equal access to education, jobs and other public services.
- Archbishop Desmond Tutu was one of the leaders who led a peaceful campaign for equal civil rights and the abolishment of apartheid, which ended in 1994.
- In the USA, black people were not allowed to attend the same schools, eat in the same restaurants or use the same swimming pools as white people.
- Dr Martin Luther King Jr became the leader of the 'Civil Rights Movement' in the USA. He campaigned for black voter registration, better housing and education for black people and the desegregation of public facilities. He was awarded the Nobel Peace Prize in 1963.

- The actions of Christians, such as Archbishop Desmond Tutu and Dr Martin Luther King Jr, with the help of others, persuaded their respective governments that racist policies were unfair and needed to be changed.

Positive discrimination

- Many people support the use of **positive discrimination** (treating people more favourably because they have been discriminated against in the past) to help people gain equal access to opportunities.
- For example, many people with physical disabilities have experienced discrimination and often do not have equal access to physical spaces. Many Christians support the use of positive discrimination, e.g. giving wheelchair users front-row positions at a football ground so they can see the match.

A Explain why Christians disagree with racial prejudice.

B 'All discrimination is wrong.'

Write a chain of reasoning in support of this statement and also for a different point of view. Include your opinion, a simple reason which you then develop and elaborate with some religious teaching.

TIP
A quote such as this is difficult to argue against. In this instance, positive discrimination could help you to come up with such an argument.

8.5 Christian teachings about wealth

RECAP

Essential information:

☐ The Old Testament teaches that wealth is a blessing from God. The New Testament teaches about the dangers associated with wealth, such as greed and selfishness.

What does the Bible say?

Belief	Teaching
In the Old Testament God blessed people with wealth in response to their faithfulness to him. This faithfulness included obeying the law he gave to Moses on behalf of the people.	66 But remember the Lord your God, for it is he who gave you the ability to produce wealth. 99 *Deuteronomy 8:18*
However, they were told that they needed to remember that their wealth was a blessing from God. This belief was reinforced by King David.	66 Wealth and honour come from you; you are the ruler of all things. 99 *1 Chronicles 29:12*
To thank God, people paid a tenth of their annual income as a **tithe** to God. A proportion of the money was shared with the poor, an action that some Christians follow by giving a tenth of their income to the Church.	66 Be sure to set aside a tenth of all that your fields produce each year. 99 *Deuteronomy 14:22*
In the New Testament wealth is associated with dangers like greed and selfishness.	66 For the love of money is a root of all sorts of evil. 99 *1 Timothy 6:10*
It is easy to become so involved with money that you neglect your spiritual life and forget to love God and love your neighbour.	66 You cannot serve both God and money. 99 *Matthew 6:24*
God's wish is for people to set their hearts on him rather than things on earth which are temporary.	66 Command those who are rich in this present world not to… put their hope in wealth which is so uncertain, but to put their hope in God, who richly provides us with everything for our enjoyment. 99 *1 Timothy 6:17*

What is the use of wealth?

- Everybody needs money to live but Christians believe that those with excess money should give it to the Church for its upkeep and mission, including providing for the poor.
- The parable of the Rich Man and Lazarus ends with the rich man in hell for not sharing his wealth with Lazarus, a poor beggar (Luke 16:19–31).
- The parable of the Sheep and the Goats states that those who help the poor are rewarded with a place in heaven (Matthew 25:31–46).
- Buddhism teaches that people create bad karma when they do not use money responsibly.
- Muslims believe that wealth is a blessing from God to be used to benefit everyone. It is only of value for the good it can do. They give 2.5% of their wealth to the mosque for the poor.

> You might be asked to compare beliefs on the uses of wealth between Christianity (the main religious tradition in Great Britain) and another religious tradition.

TIP

If you use 'for the love of money is a root of all sorts of evil', you must include 'for the love of' at the beginning otherwise you change its meaning.

APPLY

A Explain **two** religious teachings about wealth.

B Write a **developed argument** to support the idea that giving to charity should be compulsory.

Essential information:

☐ Many people throughout the world live in **poverty**, without money, food or basic needs. Most of those in extreme poverty live in Less Economically Developed Countries (LEDCs).

The problem of poverty

According to the United Nations Food and Agriculture Organisation:

- One in nine people in the world suffers from chronic hunger and is undernourished.
- Around 100 million people are homeless, with 1 billion people lacking adequate shelter or housing.
- 750 million lack access to safe water to drink and 2000 people die every day through drinking dirty water.
- Around 1 in 4 people live in conditions that harm their health, safety, prosperity and opportunities.

What are the causes of poverty?

- **Debt** – Many of the poorest countries have borrowed money from wealthy countries for such things as health care and education. These debts need to be repaid with interest, which makes the figures owed much higher.
- **Exploitation** – In the past, many poor countries that had mineral wealth were exploited by other countries who mined the minerals and paid little for them.
- **Corrupt leaders** – Some leaders of countries, often supported by richer countries, have used their country's wealth for themselves and not for their people.
- **Multinational companies** – Searching for higher profits from their goods, many very rich multinational companies manufacture products in LEDCs paying very poor wages and providing unsafe working conditions.
- **Government spending** – Many LEDCs buy weapons to fight wars in order to limit the destruction caused to their own country or to attack other countries.
- **Natural disasters** – Flooding and drought, which cause crop failure, are common in many LEDCs. Disasters such as earthquakes destroy communities and there is no money to rebuild them.

> **TIP**
> If asked about the causes of poverty, read the question carefully to check whether it specifies Britain or the world.

Poverty in Britain is not as extreme as poverty in LEDCs, but there are many people in Britain for whom life is a struggle. The causes are different from those in LEDCs. Some examples include:

- unemployment
- high cost of living
- very low wages
- gambling
- high interest rates on loans
- financial mismanagement

Responsibilities of those living in poverty

Christians believe that it is important to help those who need assistance. They do, however, encourage the poor to help themselves by improving their skills or doing voluntary work to give them experience. There are still some who are unable to find work because either:

- there are few jobs available in their area
- they lack the qualifications required and training is not available
- they are badly suited to certain jobs, or
- their domestic arrangements make full-time work impossible.

> **❝**The one who is unwilling to work shall not eat.**❞**
> *2 Thessalonians 3:10* [NIV]

APPLY

A Give **two** causes of poverty in Britain.

B 'It would be helpful if rich countries cancelled the debts of the poorest ones.'

Write your reasoned opinion about the quote.

> **TIP**
> Don't forget, you are assessed on your <u>reasoning</u>, not your opinion.

Essential information:

☐ **Exploitation** is the misuse of power or money to get others to do things for little or unfair reward.

☐ **People trafficking** is the illegal movement of people, usually for the purposes of forced labour or commercial sexual exploitation.

Fair pay

- The National Minimum Wage Act, 1998, set the lowest amount an employer can pay a worker in Britain. In 2017, the National Living Wage was set at £7.50 per hour for those over 25; it is less for younger workers.
- The majority of people in Britain earn more than the National Living Wage.

In many LEDCs, there is no such thing as a National Minimum Wage and many workers are paid a small fraction of the minimum in Britain.

▲ In 2013, this factory in Bangladesh collapsed killing over 1100 workers.

- In West Bengal, India, it is estimated that 200,000 people work on tea plantations for around £1 per day, about half of what they are entitled to.
- Some are so desperate that they are forced into work in textiles factories where they work for little reward, making clothes for wealthy countries such as Britain.
- Labour rights such as fair pay and working conditions are ignored.

Excessive interest on loans

In Britain, it is relatively easy for people, especially if employed in a job, to borrow money from a lender. For those living in poverty, however:

- Cheap loans are not available.
- There is little choice but to go to a loan company that offers small loans to be paid back quickly because of massive rates of interest, in some cases over 1000%.
- These unsecured 'payday loans' are legal in Britain but end up costing the poor vastly more than they borrow, especially if they cannot repay quickly.
- They are unlikely to be able to afford to repay a mortgage so cannot buy a house, missing out on it increasing in value and providing them with a profit.

Amount borrowed   Amount repaid

People trafficking

As the gap between the world's rich and poor widens, so the problem of human-trafficking increases.

- Moving to developed countries is attractive to those in LEDCs because the quality of life is better.
- However, they may be restricted by immigration rules preventing them from settling or working in their target country and may pay a people trafficker to transport them illegally.
- They may be found work by the trafficker with very low pay and in unsafe conditions, often in 'sweatshop' factories or in the sex industry as prostitutes.
- As they are working and living illegally, they cannot report this exploitation to the authorities.
- Some are kidnapped and forced to work as slaves or in the sex industry in another country.

APPLY

(A) Explain why some people use people traffickers.

(B) 'Developed countries requiring cheap goods are to blame for exploitation.'

Write two chains of reasoning, one supporting the statement and one supporting a different opinion. Give your opinion with a reason, develop it and elaborate it with religious teaching.

> **TIP**
> When including religious teaching, try to make it relevant and include your thoughts about it.

Essential information:

☐ Christians are guided by the key concept of justice to help the poor following Jesus' teaching to love their neighbour.

Giving aid

- There are occasions when people need help with basic needs, for example when a disaster strikes, **emergency aid** is needed.
- Voluntary aid organisations immediately mobilise their workers, many of whom are volunteers, to provide emergency supplies such as food, water, blankets, basic shelter and medical supplies.
- The money for supplies and transport comes from charitable donations.
- Providing emergency aid is just a part of the work of charitable organisations.
- **Long-term aid** is given over a long period and consists of development work designed to help those who receive it to look after their own welfare.
- An old saying, used to illustrate the meaning of long term aid, is: 'Give a man a fish and feed him for one day, teach a man to fish and feed him for life.'
- The aim is to help people to become less dependent on outside aid and be more self-reliant.

▲ UMCOR (United Methodist Committee on Relief) provides relief supplies to poverty-stricken countries.

Justice

Christians believe strongly in fairness and justice, in treating everyone fairly regardless of race, religion or nationality.

One way that justice is shown is through the Fairtrade movement, which provides long-term development opportunities based on trade.

- Fairtrade products are guaranteed to be grown and traded justly.
- Workers are paid fairly and work in good conditions.
- The price paid for the goods is a little higher than some non-Fairtrade goods but when sold in Britain, people know that they are buying a product which has not been produced by workers who are exploited.
- Profits from the sale of Fairtrade products are used to further develop communities overseas.
- Fairtrade reduces the reliance on aid and gives people self-respect.
- Fairtrade allows Christians to exercise the concept of stewardship – looking after the earth and the people living on it on behalf of God – and show their love of God and their neighbour.

In Britain, many Christians support those in need by helping in soup kitchens and food banks, and by helping charities who support the poor to find work. Christians believe that everybody has talents and abilities which they could use to get themselves out of poverty provided they have the opportunity to do so. Providing opportunities is an important part of helping people to provide for themselves.

APPLY

Ⓐ Explain **two** ways that long-term aid enables people in LEDCs to provide for themselves.

Ⓑ 'Christians don't do enough to help the poor.'

Write one paragraph supporting this view and another which expresses a different point of view. Then, in your conclusion, explain which view you believe has the strongest arguments and your reasons for this evaluation.

TIP
If writing about long-term aid, Fairtrade is a good example.

Test the 1 mark question

1. Which **one** of the following best describes prejudice?

   A Doing something to someone which is unfair

   B Misusing power to get people to do things

   C Unfairly judging someone before the facts are known

   D Using violent action to threaten or harm someone

   [1 mark]

2. Which **one** of the following is **not** an action which goes against human rights?

   A People trafficking   B Promoting tolerance   C Racial prejudice   D Exploiting the poor

   [1 mark]

Test the 2 mark question

3. Give **two** ways in which the poor are exploited.

   1) _____

   2) _____

   [2 marks]

4. Give **two** ways in which a religious person should use their wealth.

   1) _____

   2) _____

   [2 marks]

Test the 4 mark question

5. Explain **two** contrasting beliefs in contemporary British society about what role women should be allowed in worship.

   In your answer you should refer to the main religious tradition of Great Britain and one or more other religious traditions.

   [4 marks]

● **Explain one belief.**	*The main religious tradition of Great Britain is Christianity and in many denominations women are allowed to take a full and active role in leading worship.*
● Develop your explanation with more detail/an example/ reference to a religious teaching or quotation.	*For example, Libby Lane became an Anglican bishop and in the United Reformed and Methodist denominations, women are also allowed to be preachers and ministers.*
● **Explain a second contrasting belief.**	*In contrast in Islam, although men and women are seen as equals, women are believed to have been given different roles by God.*
● Develop your explanation with more detail/an example/ reference to a religious teaching or quotation.	*A woman's duty is to teach the children about Islam in the home. The imam who leads the prayers at the mosque is usually a man.*

TIP
This is a good start to the answer. It immediately identifies Christianity as the main religious religious tradition of Great Britain.

6. Explain **two** contrasting religious beliefs about prejudice based on sexuality.

   [4 marks]

● **Explain one belief.**	
● Develop your explanation with more detail/an example/ reference to a religious teaching or quotation.	
● **Explain a second contrasting belief.**	
● Develop your explanation with more detail/an example/ reference to a religious teaching or quotation.	

TIP
Do not confuse prejudice based on sexuality with gender prejudice.

8 Exam practice

7 Explain **two** similar religious beliefs about the importance of human rights. **[4 marks]**

Test the 5 mark question

8 Explain **two** religious beliefs about social justice.

Refer to sacred writings or another source of religious belief and teaching in your answer. **[5 marks]**

● **Explain one belief.**	*Jews believe social justice is important because people should be treated as equals.*
● Develop your explanation with more detail/an example.	*They believe everyone has been created in the image of God, and so people should have a fair allocation of community resources and have their human rights protected.*
● **Explain a second belief.**	*Christians believe that working to promote social justice brings them closer to God.*
● Develop your explanation with more detail/an example.	*So, many Christians have campaigned to improve human rights, for example Martin Luther King Jr, who led a peaceful movement to achieve social justice for black people who were discriminated against in America.*
● Add a reference to sacred writings or another source of religious belief and teaching. If you prefer, you can add this reference to your first belief instead.	*The parable of the Sheep and the Goats supports this Christian belief: 'Take your inheritance, the kingdom prepared for you since the salvation of the world. For I was hungry and you gave me something to drink, I was a stranger and you invited me in...' (Matthew 25:34–36)*

TIP
The parable of the Sheep and Goats is a useful story to quote when dealing with issues of justice, poverty or helping those in need.

9 Explain **two** religious beliefs about the duty to tackle poverty.

Refer to sacred writings or another source of religious belief and teaching in your answer. **[5 marks]**

● **Explain one belief.**	
● Develop your explanation with more detail/an example.	
● **Explain a second belief.**	
● Develop your explanation with more detail/an example.	
● Add a reference to sacred writings or another source of religious belief and teaching. If you prefer, you can add this reference to your first belief instead.	

10 Explain **two** religious beliefs about the dangers of wealth.

Refer to sacred writings or another source of religious belief and teaching in your answer. **[5 marks]**

Test the 12 mark question

11 'All religious believers should give to charities that help the poor.'

Evaluate this statement. In your answer you:

- should give reasoned arguments in support of this statement
- should give reasoned arguments to support a different point of view
- should refer to religious arguments
- may refer to non-religious arguments
- should reach a justified conclusion.

[12 marks]
Plus SPaG 3 ma

REASONED ARGUMENTS IN SUPPORT OF THE STATEMENT ● **Explain why some people would agree with the statement.** ● Develop your explanation with more detail and examples. ● Refer to religious teaching. Use a quote or paraphrase or refer to a religious authority. ● **Evaluate the arguments.** Is this a good argument or not? Explain why you think this.	*If all religious believers gave to charities it would go a long way to ending a lot of poverty in the world. So many people are suffering because they do not have enough money to buy food, clothes and provide a home for themselves. While a lot of food is thrown away in rich countries other people struggle to have one meal a day. Thousands have to survive on less than £1 a day. So if all religious believers were generous in their giving it would make life a lot more bearable for the poor. Some people are poor because of natural disasters or are refugees from war. They need emergency aid and religious believers should respond and it should be their duty to give to charities that are helping.*
REASONED ARGUMENTS SUPPORTING A DIFFERENT VIEW ● **Explain why some people would support a different view.** ● Develop your explanation with more detail and examples. ● Refer to religious teaching. Use a quote or paraphrase or refer to a religious authority. ● **Evaluate the arguments.** Is this a good argument or not? Explain why you think this.	*However, some religious believers are poor themselves, so will not be able to afford to help others. They are struggling to survive and have no extra money to give to charity. So you can't expect those religious believers to starve in order to give to the poor. Some may prefer to do work to help the charities like distributing and collecting envelopes for Christian Aid. Not all religious believers have to give money; they can help in other ways.*
CONCLUSION ● **Give a justified conclusion.** ● Include your own opinion together with your own reasoning. ● **Include evaluation.** Explain why you think one viewpoint is stronger than the other or why they are equally strong. ● Do not just repeat arguments you have already used without explaining how they apply to your reasoned opinion/conclusion.	*It is true that charities do a lot of good in helping those who are poor. However, it is unfair just to expect religious believers to donate money to the charities. Everyone should try and help if they can whether they are religious or not. Not all religious believers are able to donate money but they can pray or give their time to help charities.*

> **TIP**
>
> A key word in this statement is 'all'. It hints that some religious believers might <u>not</u> have a duty to give to charities. The student explains that not all believers can afford to help as some are poor themselves. The question doesn't mention money, it just says 'give to charities', so the student has rightly explained other ways people could help, for example, by helping raise money for the charity.

> **TIP**
>
> The conclusion is good because the student widens the debate to <u>all</u> people, not just religious believers. They also include a new way that believers could help – through prayer.

12 'Discrimination is always wrong.'

Evaluate this statement. In your answer you:

- should give reasoned arguments in support of this statement
- should give reasoned arguments to support a different point of view
- should refer to religious arguments
- may refer to non-religious arguments
- should reach a justified conclusion.

[12 marks]
Plus SPaG 3 marks

TIP
Don't forget that your spelling, punctuation and grammar are assessed in 12 mark questions.

REASONED ARGUMENTS IN SUPPORT OF THE STATEMENT	
• **Explain why some people would agree with the statement.** • Develop your explanation with more detail and examples. • Refer to religious teaching. Use a quote or paraphrase or refer to a religious authority. • **Evaluate the arguments.** Is this a good argument or not? Explain why you think this.	
REASONED ARGUMENTS SUPPORTING A DIFFERENT VIEW	
• **Explain why some people would support a different view.** • Develop your explanation with more detail and examples. • Refer to religious teaching. Use a quote or paraphrase or refer to a religious authority. • **Evaluate the arguments.** Is this a good argument or not? Explain why you think this.	
CONCLUSION	
• **Give a justified conclusion.** • Include your own opinion together with your own reasoning. • **Include evaluation.** Explain why you think one viewpoint is stronger than the other or why they are equally strong. • Do not just repeat arguments you have already used without explaining how they apply to your reasoned opinion/conclusion.	

13 'Everybody should have the freedom to follow whichever religion they wish to.'

Evaluate this statement. In your answer you:

- should give reasoned arguments in support of this statement
- should give reasoned arguments to support a different point of view
- should refer to religious arguments
- may refer to non-religious arguments
- should reach a justified conclusion.

[12 marks]
Plus SPaG 3 marks

Check your answers using the mark scheme on page 126. How did you do?
To feel more secure in the content you need to remember, re-read pages 106–113.
To remind yourself of what the examiner is looking for, go to pages 6–11.

Apply answers

1 Christianity: beliefs and teachings

Please note that these are suggested answers to the Apply questions, designed to give you guidance, rather than being definitive answers.

Where questions have been taken from AQA specimen papers, these suggested answers have neither been provided nor approved by AQA, nor do they constitute the only possible solutions.

1.1 **A** 'We believe in one God' (the Nicene Creed)/ first of the ten commandments. **B** *You might include*: Christians are inspired to follow the teaching of the Bible/ believe they have a relationship with God/ communicate with God through prayer/ find comfort in God in challenging times/ pray and worship/ try to follow Jesus' example.

1.2 **A** Creating humans/ caring for humans/ sending his son, Jesus, to live among humans/ requiring justice. **B** Suffering was brought into God's perfect world by Adam and Eve's disobedience/ the result of human free will/ a test of faith/ without suffering people can't show positive human qualities such as compassion/ by overcoming suffering humans learn to be strong and appreciative of good in the world. *Remember to develop each point with more detail.*

1.3 **A** 1: These persons are God the Father, the Son (Jesus) and the Holy Spirit/ these three persons are named in the Apostles Creed and the Nicene Creed. 2: God the Father is the creator of all life/ acts as a good father towards humankind, who are his children/ is omnipotent, omnibenevolent, omniscient and omnipresent. **B** *Arguments for:* 1, 2, 4, 6, 7. *Arguments against*: 3, 5, 8. *In your justified conclusion you should weigh up both sides of the argument and then say which side you personally find more convincing and why.*

1.4 **A** They value every human being as created by God/ they believe people should look after the natural world. **B** *You might conclude that this is a strong argument because it is true that Christians believe in God's omnipotence and the truth of the Bible. But you might think it is a weak argument because theories of evolution and the Big Bang are widely accepted by many Christians despite not being 'proved'. It doesn't matter whether you think the argument is weak or strong, the important thing is to carefully explain* why *you think it is weak or strong.*

1.5 **A** Jesus was God in human form/ 'The Word became flesh and made his dwelling among us' (John 1:14 [NIV])/ Jesus was born of a virgin, Mary. **B** *E.g. 'The belief that Jesus was conceived by the Holy Spirit is given in Matthew's Gospel, which says, 'His mother Mary was pledged to be married to Joseph, but before they came together, she was found to be pregnant by the Holy Spirit.''*

1.6 **A** 1: Jesus' death restored the relationship between people and God. 2: God understands human suffering because Jesus, who is God, experienced it. **B** When Jesus died he took the sins of everyone on himself (the atonement)/ if Jesus had not died he would not have risen from the dead. *The answer could be improved by developing reasons why the crucifixion is an important belief rather than merely describing what took place.*

1.7 **A** The women were told by angels that Jesus had risen/ Jesus appeared to the disciples. **B** Paul wrote, 'And if Christ has not been raised, our preaching is useless and so is your faith' (1 Corinthians 15:14 [NIV])/ 'He rose again according to the scriptures' (the Nicene Creed)/ the resurrection shows the power of good over evil and life over death/ Christians will be resurrected if they accept Jesus/ 'I look for the resurrection of the dead and the life of the world to come' (the Nicene Creed).

1.8 **A** Gives hope of life after death with Jesus/ inspires Christians to live in the way God wants. **B** *In your paragraph you should weigh up both sides of the argument and then say which side you personally find more convincing and why.*

1.9 **A** Christians believe that when they die God will judge them on their behaviour and actions during their lifetime/ as well as their faith in Jesus/ God will judge people based on how they serve others unselfishly. *Refer to the parable of the Sheep and the Goats to support your points.* **B** *You might include*: the promise of heaven inspires people to be kind to others/ people want to be with Jesus when they die so they follow his teachings/ on the other hand, no one can be sure there is an afterlife, so it is not a good way to get people to behave/ an atheist would question how a loving God could punish people forever in hell. *In your justified conclusion you should weigh up both sides of the argument and then say which side you personally find more convincing.*

1.10 **A** A loving God would not condemn people to hell/ God is forgiving so would offer everyone a second chance to repent. **B** *Arguments in support might include*: the promise of heaven would encourage good behaviour/ the threat of hell would prevent bad behaviour/ belief in heaven takes away the fear of death/ gives hope that people will experience eternal happiness even if their life on earth has been hard. *Other views might include*: atheists don't believe in heaven or hell but still have moral principles/ most people do not consider belief in the afterlife when deciding how to behave/ morality is formed in childhood by parental teaching/ if heaven and hell were made up to encourage good behaviour, it hasn't worked.

1.11 **A** Salvation by grace of God freely given through faith in Jesus/ 'For it is by grace you have been saved' (Ephesians 2:8 [NIV])/ Salvation by doing good works/ 'In the same way, faith by itself, if it is not accompanied by action, is dead' (James 2:17 [NIV]). **B** *In deciding whether you find this argument convincing, try to think of what others might say against it.*

1.12 **A** Jesus' death made up for the original sin of Adam and Eve/ Jesus' resurrection was proof that his sacrifice was accepted by God. **B** *There is no 'right' order, but suggested arguments in support*: 4, 5, 2, 8. *Arguments against*: 1, 6, 7, 3. *Missing from this evaluation is any reference to specific Christian teaching, for example a reference to sacred writing. A justified conclusion is also needed.*

2 Christianity: practices

Please note that these are suggested answers to the Apply questions, designed to give you guidance, rather than being definitive answers.

Where questions have been taken from AQA specimen papers, these suggested answers have neither been provided nor approved by AQA, nor do they constitute the only possible solutions.

2.1 **A** Private prayer/ singing hymns of praise in church. **B** *Arguments in support might include:* a set ritual is familiar to people/ provides a powerful emotional bond/ liturgical worship may be more formal, so more dramatic/ give a powerful sense of tradition. *Arguments in support of other views might include:* spontaneous worship is more powerful as it comes from the heart/ charismatic worship involves speaking in tongues so is a powerful emotional experience/ the silence of a Quaker service may be more powerful than one that uses words and hymns/ it depends on an individual Christian's point of view whether one type of service is more powerful than another.

2.2 **A** It is the prayer Jesus taught his disciples/ it is a model of good prayer as it combines praise to God with asking for one's needs. **B** *You might include an example*: a Christian may wish to pray for something personal using their own words, such as the strength to overcome an illness. *Or add a religious teaching*: Jesus said to pray in your room with the door closed so that God who sees in secret will reward you (Matthew 6:6).

2.3 **A** 1: Believers' baptism: full immersion in a pool/ person is old enough to make a mature decision about their faith. 2: Infant baptism: blessed water is poured over the baby's head/ parents and godparents make promises of faith on behalf of the child. **B** *Arguments in support might include*: at baptism the parents promise to bring up the child as a Christian so they would be lying/ it is hypocritical/ the symbolic actions have no meaning for them. *Arguments against might include*: they may not be religious themselves but that doesn't mean they should not give their child a chance to be a member of the Church/ the child receives grace at baptism regardless of their parents' future actions/ the child is cleansed from sin.

2.4 **A** 1: Christians receive God's grace/ by joining in the sacrifice of Jesus/ their faith is strengthened/ they become closer to God. 2: Communion brings the community of believers together in unity by sharing the bread and wine/ this provides support and encouragement for those going through a difficult time/ encourages church members to love others in practical ways. **B** *In your paragraph you should weigh up both sides of the argument and then say which side you personally find more convincing and why.*

2.5 **A** 1: An Orthodox Holy Communion is mainly held behind the iconostasis/ the priest distributes the consecrated bread and wine on a spoon. 2: Holy Communion in the United Reformed Church has an 'open table' so anyone can receive communion/ bread is broken and passed around the congregation/ wine is distributed in small cups. **B** *Arguments for the statement might include:* the ministry of the Word is very important because it focuses on the life and teaching of Jesus/ reminds people of sacred writing in the Old Testament/ provides spiritual education for the congregation through the sermon given by the priest/ allows the community to pray for themselves and others. *Arguments against might include*: Holy Communion services should focus on the consecration and sharing of bread and wine because that is the most important part of the service/ people receive the body and blood of Jesus/ recall Jesus' death and resurrection which saved them from sin.

2.6 1: Lourdes: pilgrims go there to seek healing, both spiritual and physical/ to help the sick bathe in the waters/ to strengthen their faith/ to take part in services with people speaking many different languages from many countries/ it is a busy place with crowds of people, unlike Iona which is quieter and more remote. 2: Iona: pilgrims wish to spend time in quiet prayer, reading the Bible or meditating/ to enjoy the natural beauty of the place so they feel closer to God who created nature/ to worship with others who are like-minded/ some prefer to feel God's presence in silence and solitude rather than in a busy place like Lourdes. **B** On a pilgrimage there are many opportunities for prayer and meditation/ for reading the scriptures/ for reflecting on one's life/ whereas on a holiday people usually spend time enjoying themselves and reading novels rather than scriptures, etc. *A Christian teaching that supports pilgrimage might include*: Jesus withdrew to a lonely place when he wanted to pray/ Bernadette was told by Mary in a vision to build a church in Lourdes and pray for sinners, so Christians are following their traditional teaching by going there.

2.7 **A** By attending services which emphasise Jesus is risen/ by celebrating with family and friends/ giving Easter eggs to children to symbolise new life. **B** *Arguments for might include*: Christmas is very commercialised/ many people think about food, presents and seeing their relatives, not about Jesus/ not many people go to church on Christmas/ some think that in multicultural Britain, celebrating Christmas as a religious festival might offend others. *Arguments against might include*: Christmas is still a religious holiday in Britain/ the royal family go to church on Christmas Day and many Christians attend Midnight Mass/ carol services are held to prepare for the coming of Jesus into the world/ schools have nativity plays about Jesus' birth and often collect presents to give to children who are less fortunate.

2.8 **A** 1: The community of Christians/ holy people of God/ Body of Christ. 2: A building in which Christians worship. **B** The Church is the Body of Christ and as such has a duty to help the needy/ Christians are taught to love their neighbour/ the parable of the Sheep and the Goats/ the parable of the Good Samaritan.

2.9 **A** Patrol streets in urban areas to support vulnerable people/ challenge gang and knife crime/ listen to people's problems/ help young people who have had too much to drink and may end up in trouble/ try to stop anti-social behaviour/ in this way they show love of neighbour/ 'Faith by itself, if it is not accompanied by action, is dead' (James 2:17 [NIV]). **B** *Two religious arguments might include:* Jesus taught that Christians should help others by showing agape love towards them/ this means being unselfish, caring and putting others' needs before your own, including praying for your neighbours' needs/ Jesus taught Christians should give practical help to others in the Parable of the Sheep and the Goats/ he said to feed the hungry, clothe the naked, etc. *Two non-religious arguments against the statement might include:* praying is pointless/ not a practical action/ no one will know if prayer works to help them/ Christians should not have to be street pastors or social workers/ it is the police and social services' responsibility, not the Church's responsibility.

2.10 A By telling non-believers that Jesus Christ, the Son of God, came into the world as its saviour/ by spreading the Christian faith through evangelism. **B** *Arguments for:* 1, 3, 5. *Arguments against:* 2, 4, 6. *You should weigh up both sides of the argument and then say which side you personally find more convincing.*

2.11 A Through organisations that promote evangelism, such as Christ for all Nations/ through personal witness and example. **B** *You should weigh up the argument and suggest how it could be improved – e.g. by referring to the Great Commission (which suggests all Christians have a duty to spread the gospel), or by considering arguments for the statement.*

2.12 A 1: The Church works on a personal level to try to restore relationships between individuals/ between conflicting groups in the community. 2: The Church has sponsored different organisations that work for reconciliation/ e.g. the Irish Churches Peace Project. **B** Jesus taught, 'Love the Lord your God with all your heart and with all your soul and with all your mind. This is the great and first commandment.' (Matthew 22: 37–38 [NIV])/ therefore reconciliation to God is most important/ reconciliation to one's neighbour is second: 'Love your neighbour as yourself' (Matthew 22:39 [NIV]).

2.13 A Smuggling Bibles into the USSR to give comfort to persecuted Christians/ sending money to projects that support persecuted Christians. **B** *A religious argument might include:* it is possible for a Christian to be happy even in times of persecution because they believe they are sharing in the sufferings of Jesus/ their courage can inspire others to become Christians/ persecution strengthens their faith. *A non-religious argument might include:* no one can be happy while being persecuted/ they may be angry at the injustice of their treatment and turn to violence or stop believing in God.

2.14 A 1: Emergency relief includes food, shelter and water to people suffering from a natural disaster or sudden war/ parables such as the Rich Man and Lazarus and the Good Samaritan encourage Christians to help the needy. 2: Long-term aid may include education or new farming equipment that helps to make people independent of aid/ 'If anyone has material possessions and sees a brother or sister in need but has no pity on them, how can the love of God be in that person?' (1 John 3:17 [NIV]). **B** *Arguments for the statement might include:* religious charities can respond quickly to emergencies but it is not their role to provide long-term aid/ the countries themselves should be helping their own people/ long-term aid might make people dependent on religious charities. *Arguments against might include:* religious charities should provide long-term aid because people are still in need/ it will give independence eventually/ it is better to teach people how to make a living for themselves than merely to feed them for a short period of time/ the Parable of the Sheep and the Goats teaches that God will judge people on whether they have helped their fellow humans because helping them is helping Jesus Christ.

3 Relationships and families

Please note that these are suggested answers to the Apply questions, designed to give you guidance, rather than being definitive answers.

3.1 A It is the relationship between the two people, not their gender that is important/ the relationship should show Christian qualities of love, commitment, faithfulness, etc./ *on the other hand,* God's plan for humans was heterosexual relationships/ 'Be fruitful and increase in number…' (Genesis 1:28 [NIV]). **B** *An example of a religious argument:* Christians believe sex expresses a deep, lifelong union and casual sex does not represent this. *An example of a non-religious argument:* the acceptance of contraception and legal abortion has made casual sex more common.

3.2 A 'You shall not commit adultery' (Exodus 20:14 [NIV]). **B** *In support:* it can be a valid expression of love for each other/ the couple may intend to marry but just can't afford it at the time. *Against:* 'your bodies are temples of the Holy Spirit' (1 Corinthians 6:19 [NIV])/ the Church teaches that sex requires the commitment of marriage. *A development may be:* the Catholic Church teaches that sex should be open to the possibility of creating new life/ having sex before marriage risks pregnancy.

3.3 A Catholic and Orthodox Churches believe the use of contraception within marriage goes against the natural law/ other Christian churches accept its use e.g. to avoid harming the mother's health. **B** *The argument is weak because it does not give specific reasons why the Church should be able to take a view about family planning. It could be improved by saying e.g. 'If the Church did not take a view on family planning then they would be ignoring teachings in the Bible related to sex and marriage (e.g. Genesis 1:28 and 2:24).'*

3.4 A 'That is why a man leaves his father or mother and is united to his wife, and they become one flesh' (Genesis 2:24 [NIV]). **B** Marriage is a legal contract/ society is more stable if the rights of all people are protected/ 'The Church sees marriage between a man and a woman, as central to the stability and health of human society' (House of Bishops of the General Synod of the Church of England).

3.5 A 1: The Catholic Church teaches that marriage is a sacrament between two baptised people that is permanent and cannot be dissolved. 2: Although not the Christian ideal, divorce can be justified e.g. if the children are at risk of abuse. **B** *For:*

children are badly affected by divorce/ marriage is a sacrament and reflects the love Christ has for his Church/ Jesus taught that anyone who divorced and remarried was committing adultery (Mark 10:11–12). *Against:* continual arguments or abuse can damage children more than divorce/ atheists and humanists do not believe vows are made before God/ some Christians think the Church should reflect God's forgiveness and allow couples a second chance for happiness.

3.6 A It is in the family that a child learns to love/ a Christian family is where a child learns faith in God and Jesus. **B** 1: Christians must 'love one another'/ it is in the family that a child learns how to love others and to receive love/ Christians believe God is love, therefore raise their children with love so that they come to know God, etc. 2: Religious parents are expected to bring their children up in their faith/ it is a Christian parent's duty to teach their children right from wrong/ without love, children will not take notice of these lessons/ will lack security and stability in their lives, etc.

3.7 A 1: When children are little, they are taught right from wrong/ 'Honour your father and your mother…' (Exodus 20:12 [NIV]). 2: Many Christian parents present their babies for baptism/ teach them to pray/ some send them to faith schools. **B**: *You should weigh up both sides of the argument and then say which side you personally find more convincing.*

3.8 A All people are created equal in the image of God/ the command to love one's neighbour as oneself shows that discrimination is wrong. **B** Paul taught that this was wrong when he said, 'There is neither… male nor female, for you are all one in Christ Jesus' (Galatians 3:28 [NIV]).

4 Religion and life

Please note that these are suggested answers to the Apply questions, designed to give you guidance, rather than being definitive answers.

4.1 A 1: The world was created by God/ in six days, with one day's rest/ as described in Genesis, which is literally true/ the days could be longer periods of time. 2: The creation stories are symbolic/ God's creation is the main message/ science may help people understand how God created the universe. **B** *For:* the Genesis story must be literally true because Bible is the word of God, so it is not possible to believe the Big Bang theory/ there is no God so the Big Bang theory is the only option/ science knows more than religion does. *Against:* if the Genesis story is not read literally then it is possible to believe in both/ the Big Bang theory explains the method God used/ the Big Bang was triggered by God and not by random chance.

4.2 A Looking after something on behalf of somebody else, e.g. looking after the earth for God. **B** Stewardship means looking after/ a God-given duty and responsibility/ not being stewards is letting God down/ the emphasis is on care not domination or exploitation/ gives humans a role and justifies them being allowed to stay on earth.

4.3 A Pollution causes harm to living things including humans/ not good stewardship and therefore against God's wishes (Genesis 1:28)/ may lead to God's fair judgement being harsh (the parable of talents)/ pollution is not loving to each other or to God (Luke 10:27). **B** *E.g. 'This means they should take care not to use vehicles that cause the most pollution, dispose of their waste in a way that does not harm the earth, and recycle where possible. If humans use their talents wrongly, for example by not helping to stop pollution, God's judgement on them when they die may be harsher than they expect. This is shown in the Parable of the Talents which Jesus taught.'*

4.4 A Do not like the taste of meat/ prevents cruelty to animals/ it is healthier/ breeding animals to kill them for food is poor stewardship. **B** All killing of living beings is cruel/ animals bred for experimentation have no freedom in their lives/ there are alternatives that are not harmful to animals/ the Bible says humans should care for animals (e.g. Proverbs 12:10)/ experimenting on animals is not good stewardship.

4.5 A 1: Human life was created last/ life was breathed into Adam by God/ humans have the duty to look after the earth/ Eve was created by God from Adam/ created in God's image. 2: Life started with single-celled creatures in the sea/ evolved into creatures living on land/ creatures resembling humans evolved around 2.5 million years ago/ survival of the fittest. **B** *Once opinion is given, i.e. agreement with Genesis, science or a combination of both, and two reasons to support it which may be based on the answers for 4.6 A, perhaps with further content on the existence and/or role of God.*

4.6 A The pregnancy endangers the woman's life/ the woman's physical or mental health is endangered/ there is a strong risk the baby will be born with severe disabilities/ an additional child may endanger the health of other children in the family/ within the first 24 weeks of pregnancy/ must be decided by at least two doctors. **B** *For:* being brought up with a poor quality of life is not loving/ possibly not the child's preferred option had they been able to choose. *Against:* preventing life is never the best option/ the sanctity of life/ the family should be supported to improve the child's quality of life/ better a poor quality of life than no life.

4.7 A Drugs used to end life are God-given/ free will to end life/ most loving and compassionate thing to do/ may allow a painless death/ Hindus believe that suffering may be caused by bad karma in another life/ suffering must be endured/ ahimsa does not allow any harm to be caused/ carrying out euthanasia causes bad karma. **B** *See answers to 4.7 A for arguments to support the statement. Arguments against may include:* it is murder/ 'You shall not murder.' (Exodus 20:13 [NIV])/ interferes with God's plan/ open to abuse/ disrespects the sanctity of life/ only God should take life/ suffering can bring a person closer to God and help them understand Jesus' suffering.

4.8 A Accept Jesus is Lord and believe that Jesus rose from the dead (Romans 10:9)/ believe that Jesus opened the way to heaven/ have faith that Jesus can forgive sin if asked/ follow the teachings of Jesus and the Church. **B** Heaven and hell are places of God and the devil, neither of which exist/ literal descriptions of both are hard to believe (e.g. Matthew 13:50)/ a good God would not allow hell as a place of punishment/ Christians cannot agree on the details or process (e.g. purgatory, what the afterlife will be like).

5 The existence of God and revelation

Please note that these are suggested answers to the Apply questions, designed to give you guidance, rather than being definitive answers.

5.1 A The earth and humans were created for a purpose/ the intricacy and complexity of earth shows it cannot have appeared by chance/ the designer can only have been God/ the thumb is evidence of design because it allows precise delicate movement/ everything in the universe is in a regular order so must have been designed/ everything in the universe is perfect to sustain life. **B** *See the answers to 5.1 A for arguments to agree with the statement. Arguments against could include*: natural selection happens by chance/ species are developed by evolution, not a designer/ suffering proves there is no designer God/ order and structure in nature is imposed by humans, not God.

5.2 A Everything (including the universe) has a cause to explain its existence/ to cause everything to exist there must be something existing that is eternal and without a cause/ this can only be God/ so God must exist/ this means God caused everything to exist, possibly by causing the Big Bang. **B** *See the answers to 5.2 A for arguments to agree with the statement. Arguments against could include*: what caused God?/ the universe may be eternal, not God/ the universe may not need a cause/ the Big Bang was random chance.

5.3 A As science cannot explain miracles, they must be caused by something outside nature/ the only thing that exists outside nature is God/ therefore miracles must be the work of God. **B** *E.g. 'There is never enough evidence to prove that miracles are the work of God, instead of having a (perhaps unknown) scientific explanation. People who claim to have witnessed miracles are making them up or mistaken about what they have experienced. On the other hand, anyone who has witnessed a miracle is unlikely to remember it wrongly and there are 69 recorded miracles at Lourdes alone. They cannot all have been remembered wrongly. If Jesus had not performed miracles, they wouldn't have been written down in the Bible, and people who were there at the time would have spoken out if they thought the miracles were made up.'*

5.4 A *Reasons might include*: if God was loving, he would not allow suffering/ evil exists because God does not/ an all-knowing and all-powerful God would know about suffering and do something to prevent it. *Counter-arguments might include*: suffering is caused by wrong use of free will which God gifted to humans/ without evil, there would be no good/ suffering allows others to show love and compassion. **B** *E.g. 'Science challenges the existence of God because it gives explanations for things that used to be explained with God, which means God is no longer needed as the answer to these things. For example, some people would say the Big Bang theory removes the need to believe that God created the universe. However, others believe science can help to explain God's creation. For example, the Big Bang theory explains how God created the universe, and the theory of evolution explains how God brought life to earth and developed it to what it is like now.'*

5.5 A A specific experience of God such as a dream, vision, prophecy or miracle. Any example from scripture, tradition, history or the present day can be given. **B** *E.g. 'I disagree with this statement because visions can have a profound effect on people's lives, which would be unlikely to happen if they were not real. For example, Saul converted to Christianity after he saw a blinding light and heard Jesus' voice. The way he changed his life as a result of this vision means it probably did happen. Also, he certainly did not expect to experience God in this way because he was very opposed to Christianity.'*

5.6 A By gaining greater insight about God from events in nature/ e.g. the natural world reveals God to be creative, all-knowing and powerful/ by learning about God's past actions through reading scripture/ by learning about God's relationship with people through reading scripture/ the Bible reveals God to be powerful, just, loving and forgiving. **B** *E.g. 'The world has changed so much over the past 2000 years that the Bible is no longer relevant to the modern world. It is also impossible to know how accurate it is because it was written so long ago. It is unreliable and out-of-date, so cannot be relied on to help people believe in God.'*

5.7 A *Drawing of a symbol for each of the seven ideas about God.* **B** E.g. *'I agree with the statement because God is unique. God's nature is outside the comprehension of any other being because nobody but God is all-powerful, all-knowing or eternal. Humans and other beings are subject to limits that God is not, so they cannot possibly be like him. On the other hand, it is possible for people to display some of the same qualities that God has, although not so perfectly. For example, God is benevolent, and people can also show love and kindness towards others. God is also personal, which means he has 'human' characteristics – so this means humans and God do share some of the same qualities.'*

5.8 A Drugs or alcohol can make a person lose touch with reality/ wishful thinking means people can persuade themselves that something has happened purely because they want it to/ hallucinations can be symptoms of some illnesses/ some people might lie to become famous or rich, as it is hard to disprove their lies/ some may genuinely believe they have had a revelation but there may be a perfectly normal explanation that they do not know about. **B** *E.g. 'There is no way to prove that a revelation means God does exist. There are perfectly normal explanations for what people say are revelations, so they cannot be considered as evidence for God. For example, they might just be hallucinations caused by illness, or made up by someone to get attention. There is no way to know if a person's 'revelation' is genuine or not, so it cannot act as proof that God exists.'*

6 Religion, peace and conflict

Please note that these are suggested answers to the Apply questions, designed to give you guidance, rather than being definitive answers.

6.1 A The Lord's Prayer says, 'Forgive us our sins as we forgive those who sin against us'/ this means God expects Christians to forgive others if they wish to receive God's mercy/ Jesus told people to 'turn the other cheek' when people hurt them. **B** *Arguments for*: the Church teaches that killing is wrong/ Jesus' teaching does not support war/ Jesus told people to love their enemies. *Arguments against*: Christians believe in the just war theory/ it is sometimes necessary to take part in war for self-defence/ war can help create a more just and fair society (e.g. if it is being used to end an oppressive dictatorship).

6.2 A There is an injustice/ they believe in loving their neighbours. **B** *You might wish to use recent terrorist attacks as examples*/ 'You shall not murder' (Exodus 20:13 [NIV]).

6.3 A d) Forgiveness. **B** *Read the statements carefully. You should weigh up both sides of the argument and then say which side you personally find more convincing.*

6.4 A *Beliefs must be contrasting*. All religions are against the use of weapons of mass destruction/ Christians believe life is sacred (sanctity of life)/ only God has the right to end life/ God created the earth and it should not be destroyed with WMD/ nothing can justify the use of WMDs which target innocent people/ some people agree with the possession of nuclear weapons as a deterrent/ to maintain peace and prevent attack/ some people think the use of nuclear weapons in war can be justified/ e.g. they ended the Second World War. **B** 'You shall not murder' (Exodus 20:13 [NIV])/ only God has the right to end life/ sanctity of life.

6.5 A Just cause/ proper legal authority/ just intention/ last resort/ chance of success/ proportional. **B** *For*: the just war theory says war should be a last resort/ all other means of settling disputes should be tried first/ limited retaliation is accepted by some Christians based on the teaching about 'eye for eye, tooth for tooth' (Exodus 21:24 [NIV]). *Against*: Quakers believe war is never justified/ Jesus taught that even the anger that leads to violence is wrong (Matthew 5: 21–22)/ Jesus did not try to resist arrest and told Peter to put his sword away.

6.6 A Fighting for God or a religious cause/ authorised by a high religious authority. **B** *Arguments in support might include*: in a democracy people are entitled to freedom of speech/ there is no need to turn to violence to defend religion/ religious freedoms are guaranteed by Human Rights legislation. *Other views might include*: if a particular religious group is constantly attacked, they may feel justified in using violent means to respond/ however this is not what is meant by 'holy war.'

6.7 A 1: Quakers are a Christian denomination that strongly supports pacifism/ some Christians were conscientious objectors in the Second World War/ 'Blessed are the peacemakers' (Matthew 5:9 [NIV]). 2: these Christians believe in the just war theory/ although peace is the ideal, it cannot always be achieved/ in the face of great evil (e.g. Nazism) war is sometimes necessary. **B** Promoting justice and human rights is the best way of preventing conflict because (1) conflict is often caused by injustice/ if people feel that their rights are being denied they may wish to take violent action to achieve equality of opportunity/ for example, racist laws in some countries provoked violent clashes with the authorities, etc. (2) It is better to make sure people are treated with equal dignity and respect so that conflict is avoided / Christians believe all human beings are created by God so should be treated fairly / Christian charities like Christian Aid and Caritas help the poor to rise out of poverty and campaign to establish human rights in the hope that wars will not be necessary to bring about justice, etc.

6.8 A By raising money to help refugees through organisations such as Caritas and Christian Aid/ by going to war-torn areas to deliver emergency supplies to victims. **B** *Read the statements carefully. You should weigh up both sides of the argument and then say which side you personally find more convincing, giving reasons why.*

7 Religion, crime and punishment

Please note that these are suggested answers to the Apply questions, designed to give you guidance, rather than being definitive answers.

7.1 A Nobody is evil/ all humans make mistakes/ original sin gave humans the tendency to do wrong things/ usually there is a reason for wrongdoing as humans are created good/ people committing evil actions should be punished. **B** *For the statement*: intentions are the reasons for actions/ loving and compassionate intentions usually bring about good actions/ 'But I tell you that anyone who looks at a woman lustfully has already committed adultery with her in his heart' (Matthew 5:28 [NIV]). *Against the statement*: nobody is helped or harmed by intentions but they may be by actions / 'faith by itself, if it is not accompanied by action, is dead' (James 2:17 [NIV]).

7.2 A Poverty can lead people to steal food/ a person's upbringing may lead them to view crime as acceptable/ people may break a law in order to protest against it/ greed may prompt someone to steal something they want. **B** Addiction takes away choice/ a person may need to commit crimes to fund their addiction/ addiction may cause illegal actions because the offender doesn't realise what they are doing/ addicts should be helped to defeat their addiction so they do not commit crimes/ there is no good reason for committing crimes/ some other reasons (e.g. poverty and mental illness) are also good reasons for committing crimes.

7.3 A Hate crimes usually involve violence and possibly killing/ murder is unlawful killing/ hate crimes result from prejudice, murder can have other reasons/ murder is generally considered to be worse/ some murders are classed as hate crimes. **B** *For*: hatred of a criminal is not constructive/ reasons why the criminal committed the crime should be considered/ love and compassion are religious teachings that should extend even to criminals. *Against*: criminal actions can cause great harm and upset/ some victims never fully recover from a criminal action/ 'let everyone be subject to the governing authorities, for there is no authority except that which God established' (Romans 13:1 [NIV])/ crimes break Christian teachings and morality.

7.4 **A** *Retribution*: getting your own back/ the offender should receive the same (not greater) injuries and harm that their actions caused. *Deterrence*: putting people off from committing crimes/ the punishment should be severe enough to prevent repetition of the offence. *Reformation*: changing someone's behaviour for the better/ offenders are helped to change so they do not reoffend. **B** *For*: severe punishment can help prevent future crimes/ the criminal deserves severe punishment for what they have done/ 'eye for an eye' means punishment should equal harm caused, so more serious crimes deserve severe punishment. *Against*: less severe punishment may lead more easily to repentance and change/ positive methods (e.g. reformation) are more likely to have a lasting effect/ 'Do not take revenge, my dear friends' (Romans 12:19 [NIV]).

7.5 **A** Free will is given by God to allow humans to make their own choices and decisions/ it does not mean humans can choose to do whatever they want; there are good or bad consequences to every action/ Christian beliefs and teachings encourage the responsible use of free will, as does the law and human conscience. **B** *For*: all violence causes suffering/ violence is not loving and doesn't show respect, even in self-defence/ better to try to repair damage that has been done rather than responding with further violence/ Jesus gave an example during his arrest when he healed the High Priest's servant. *Against*: using violence in self-defence may cause less harm than allowing an attack to continue/ e.g. the use of atom bombs helped to end the Second World War.

7.6 **A** Christians oppose all punishment that causes harm to offenders/ corporal punishment has no element of reform/ it is inhumane/ negative. **B** Christians believe in compassion and 'love your neighbour' so criminals should be treated well/ all humans are deserving of respect as they are created by God/ 'eye for an eye' suggests offenders who commit serious crimes should receive severe punishment/ God is sometimes pictured as a harsh but fair judge.

7.7 **A** Christians should forgive a person no matter what they have done/ Jesus said there is no limit to the number of times a person should forgive/ Jews believe the offender should show remorse and ask for forgiveness/ only then can the offender expect to be forgiven by God/ Muslims believe only God can truly forgive, and only when he knows the offender is truly sorry and intends to follow the faith properly/ the offender should seek forgiveness from the victim before expecting God to forgive them. **B** *E.g. 'I agree that nobody should expect to be forgiven more than once because they should have learned from their original mistake. If they were punished on the first occasion they should have used the chance to repent and promised not to offend again. On the other hand, Christians are taught they should forgive again. When asked how many times they should forgive, Jesus said, 'not seven times, but seventy-seven times.' Because of this Christians should forgive as many times as necessary, even if the offender does not expect it. They should also try to help the offender not to commit offences in future.'*

7.8 **A** Some Bible passages agree with retribution (e.g. Genesis 9:6)/ others with reform (e.g. Ezekiel 33:11)/ 'You shall not murder' (Exodus 20:13 [NIV])/ death penalty does not reform the offender, which Christians believe is an important aim/ does not respect the sanctity of life. **B** The death penalty is not loving or compassionate/ may kill an innocent person by mistake/ life is sacred and only God has the right to take it/ evidence suggests that it does not deter/ a dead offender cannot be reformed/ the victim's family may not want it to happen.

8 Religion, human rights and social justice

Please note that these are suggested answers to the Apply questions, designed to give you guidance, rather than being definitive answers.

8.1 **A** *Amos 5:24*: work towards and look forward to a time when justice and righteousness exist/ *Romans 13:1*: God gives the ruling authorities the right to exist, so their rules should be obeyed/ *Mark 12:31*: it is a Christians duty to help others out of love and compassion/ *James 2:20*: if faith makes no difference to how a person lives then it is useless. **B** *For*: everyone is entitled to have rights/ they allow the more disadvantaged to be treated with justice and compassion/ promote equality/ allow people freedom to live their lives as they wish. *Against*: some people (e.g. murderers) do not deserve rights/ rights should be earned/ those who do not respect the rights of others should have no rights themselves.

8.2 **A** All prejudice is unacceptable/ even if homosexuality is believed to be sinful, it shouldn't be seen as a reason for prejudice/ all sexual orientations are natural and morally acceptable/ any sexual relationship based on love is good. **B** *For*: traditional Christian views on gender are often seen as sexist/ 'Women should remain silent in the churches' (1 Corinthians 14:34 [NIV])/ leadership of the church has traditionally been male. *Against*: Jesus treated women as equal to men/ women can now become priests in the Church of England/ giving women different roles in the Church is not necessarily sexist.

8.3 **A** The right to believe and practise whatever religion a person chooses without interference or hindrance. **B** It is a basic human right to be allowed to follow a faith/ following any faith can only be helpful to a person and society as a whole/ some sects and interpretations of major faiths may be harmful and so should be avoided.

8.4 **A** It is unjust/ denies belief in equality/ harmful/ illegal/ 'there is neither Jew nor Gentile, neither slave nor free, nor is there male and female for you are one in Christ Jesus' (Galatians 3:28)/ not loving or compassionate/ against the will of God, etc. **B** *E.g. 'I believe all discrimination is wrong because it can cause great harm to people. It is also completely unjust because Christians believe that all humans of all races are created by God, in his image, and with equal rights. Treating people of some races badly shows no love and respect to them and makes them feel that they are in some way inferior and wrong through no fault of their own. However, positive discrimination is an exception because it is not harmful. This means to treat people of some minority groups better than others, for example by giving disabled people special areas of seating in sports stadiums and theatres. This allows them equal opportunity to see sports or arts performances because it removes problems with access. Another example is giving women a better chance of becoming an MP because there have never been as many female MPs as male. Christians see this as fulfilling the prophecy of Amos: 'Let justice roll on like a river and righteousness like a never-failing stream' (Amos 5:24).'*

8.5 **A** God blesses people with wealth/ excess wealth should be shared with those who have less/ wealth can be dangerous (1 Timothy 6:10)/ can cause neglect of the spiritual life (Matthew 6:24). **B** *E.g. 'Charities are desperate for money so they can carry out their work. They rely on people's generosity to give them money. If giving to charity was compulsory, it is likely they would receive more than they do at present, so could help more people in need throughout the world. Some Christians pay a tithe of 10% of their earnings to the Church or charity and more people should do this.'*

8.6 **A** Unemployment/ low wages/ high cost of living/ debt from loans or credit cards/ gambling/ addiction/ financial mismanagement. **B** *For*: rich countries can afford to write off the debts/ poor countries that need to borrow for their country to survive cannot afford to repay debts/ paying rich countries back could cost in lives the poorest countries, who need the money for other things. *Against*: if debts were cancelled, poor countries might think they can always borrow money without any consequences/ this might lead to reckless management of finances/ rich countries need money too.

8.7 **A** They are desperate to start a new life in a safer and more wealthy country/ they cannot cross the sea on their own/ they have no legal right to enter another country so have to do it illegally. **B** *E.g. 'Developed countries that prefer to buy cheap goods do cause exploitation. In order to have cheap goods, the cost of making them has to be reduced to a minimum. This means exploiting workers by paying them next to nothing. If people in developed countries were prepared to pay a little more, the workers could be paid more. Exploitation goes against religious ideas of justice, compassion and love, and shows that Amos' vision that justice should flow like a river and righteousness like a stream has not yet been reached. However, another opinion is that it is the multinational companies that make the goods, and the shops that sell the goods, who are to blame. Designer goods are often made in poor countries by people who are exploited, yet they are expensive to buy because the producers and shops are keen to make ever bigger profits because they are so greedy. In 1 Timothy it says, 'the love of money is the root of all evil', so exploitation of poor countries is caused by the greed of rich people, not poor people who want to buy decent things at prices they can afford.'*

8.8 **A** Long-term aid educates people in skills such as literacy, numeracy and basic training to allow them to access work/ teaches them agricultural methods to grow their own crops/ provides assistance for setting up a small business to earn enough to provide for their needs. **B** The fact that so many people are still poor shows that much more still needs to be done/ some religions do not set a good example to believers because they invest a lot of wealth in places of worship rather than giving it to the poor/ 'If a man will not work, he shall not eat' (2 Thessalonians 3:10)/ many Christians do all they can to help the poor/ Christians may be poor themselves so they don't have the money to spare/ some could help out more in practical ways if they cannot afford to give much/ the fact so many people are still poor shows that much more still needs to be done.

Exam practice answers

1 Beliefs and teachings

Test the 1 mark question

1. B) Incarnation

2. C) Benevolent

Test the 2 mark question

Suggested answers, other relevant answers would be credited. 1 mark for each correct point.

3. Through good works/ through the grace of God/ through faith/ through Jesus' death/ through obeying the Ten Commandments/ through loving one's neighbour/ through prayer/ through worship/ through the Holy Spirit.

4. Christians believe everyone will be raised from the dead (resurrection)/ face judgement of God/ immediately or at the end of time/ Judgement Day/ Second Coming of Christ/ Jesus rose from the dead/ people will be judged on how they lived their lives/ sent to heaven, hell or purgatory/ resurrection of the body/ restoration to glorified bodies.

Test the 4 mark question

Suggested answers, other relevant answers would be credited. 1 mark for each simple contrasting or similar point, another mark for developing each point, so a maximum of 4 marks for two developed points.

6. Christians may show respect towards all of God's creation/ actively work for conservation/ show stewardship/ take practical steps like recycling/ be energy efficient.

Christians may treat others with respect/ all are created 'in imago dei' (in God's image)/ work for peace between people/ support charities that help people in need/ reflect God in all they do.

Christians may take care of themselves (both body and soul)/ adopt healthy lifestyles/ develop spiritual practices/ prayer/ worship/ meditation.

7. Christians believe that because God is loving, God wants the best for them/ they accept God's will as being for their benefit, even if it does not appear to be so/ they love others because God loves them.

God's greatest act of love was sending his Son Jesus/ to save people from sin/ to gain eternal life/ so they are grateful to God/ express their thanks through worship or praise.

God is love/ qualities of love described in Paul's letter to the Corinthians/ patient/ kind/ not easily angered/ Christians try to live according to these descriptions of love.

Test the 5 mark question

Suggested answers, other relevant answers would be credited. 1 mark for each simple contrasting or similar belief, another mark for developing each belief, so 4 marks for two developed beliefs, 1 extra mark for a correct reference to a source of religious belief or teaching.

9. Christians believe God is omnipotent (all-powerful)/ has supreme authority/ can do all things/ 'Nothing is impossible with God' (Luke 1:37 [NIV])/ is loving (benevolent)/ wants good for God's creation/ wants people to love God freely in return/ 'God so loved the world that he gave his one and only Son, that whoever believes in him shall not perish but have eternal life' (John 3:16 [NIV])/ is just (fair/righteous)/ wants people to choose good over evil/ punishes wrongdoing/ is the perfect judge of human character.

Christians believe there is only one God/ 'The Lord is our God, the Lord alone' (Deuteronomy 6:4 [NIV])/ but within God there is a Trinity of persons/ Father, Son (Jesus), Holy Spirit/ 'Our Father in heaven' (Lord's Prayer)/ the Spirit's presence at Jesus' baptism.

God is the creator of all that is/ 'In the beginning, God created the heavens and the earth' (Genesis 1:1 [NIV])/ the Spirit was present at creation/ the Word of God (the Son) was involved in creation too.

10. Christians believe Jesus restored the relationship between God and humanity/ Jesus atoned for the sins of humankind/ God accepted his death as atonement for sin by raising Jesus from the dead/ 'Jesus Christ [...] is the atoning sacrifice for our sins, and not only for ours but also for the sins of the whole world' (1 John 2: 1–2 [NIV]).

Through the atonement of Jesus, humans can receive forgiveness for sin/ be able to get close to God/ gain eternal life/ sin has been defeated/ 'For the wages of sin is death, but the gift of God is eternal life in Christ Jesus our Lord' (Romans 6:23 [NIV]).

Jesus' death atoned for the original sin of Adam and Eve/ Adam chose to disobey God, but Jesus chose to offer his life as a sacrifice/ 'For since death came through a man, the resurrection of the dead also comes through a man. For as in Adam all die, so in Christ all will be made alive' (1 Corinthians 15:21 [NIV]).

Test the 12 mark question

Suggested answers shown here, but see page 10 for guidance on levels of response.

12. **Arguments in support**

• Hell is not a place/ exploration of the earth and space have not discovered a place where spirits are punished forever/ although hell is shown in paintings as a place of fire and torture ruled by Satan (the devil) somewhere beneath the earth, no such place exists.

• The idea of hell is inconsistent with a benevolent God/ Christians believe God is loving/ a loving God would never send anyone to eternal damnation in hell/ like a loving Father, God will give people another chance if they repent.

• The idea of hell is just a way of comforting those who want to see justice/ some people get away with many bad things and seem not to receive punishment in this life/ the idea of hell ensures the idea of justice being done, but it does not really exist.

Arguments in support of other views

• Today hell is more often thought to be an eternal state of mind being cut off from the possibility of God/ the state of being without God, rather than a place/ a person who did not acknowledge God or follow his teachings would necessarily end up without God in the afterlife.

• Christians believe God is just/ it is only fair that someone who has gone against God's laws should be punished eventually/ it is a just punishment for an immoral life.

• Jesus spoke about hell as a possible consequence for sinners/ 'But I tell you that anyone who is angry with a brother or sister will be subject to judgment [...] And anyone who says, "You fool!" will be in danger of the fire of hell.' (Matthew 5:22 [NIV])/ 'If your right eye causes you to stumble, gouge it out and throw it away. It is better for you to lose one part of your body than for your whole body to be thrown into hell.' (Matthew 5:29 [NIV])/ 'For if God did not spare angels when they sinned, but sent them to hell, putting them in chains of darkness to be held for judgment' (2 Peter 2:4 [NIV]).

13. **Arguments in support**

• Salvation means deliverance from sin and admission to heaven brought about by Jesus/ saving one's soul/ sin separates people from God who is holy/ the original sin of Adam and Eve brought suffering and death to humankind/ so God gave the law so that people would know how to stay close to him/ Jesus' teaching takes the law even further.

• One way of gaining salvation is through good works/ by having faith in God and obeying God's laws/ obeying the Ten Commandments (Exodus 20:1–19) is the best way of being saved because by doing so the Christian is avoiding sin/ following other Christian teachings such as the Beatitudes (Matthew 5:1–12) helps gain salvation through good works/ being merciful/ a peacemaker.

• Christians believe God gave people free will to make moral choices/ following God's law shows the person is willing to use their free will wisely.

Arguments in support of other views

• The best way of gaining salvation is through grace/ grace is a free gift of God's love and support/ it is not earned by following laws/ faith in Jesus is all a person needs to be saved/ 'For it is by grace you have been saved, through faith – and this is not from yourselves, it is the gift of God – not by works, so that no one can boast.' (Ephesians 2:8–9 [NIV]).

• Merely following the law is a legalistic approach/ it can hide sinfulness inside a person/ Jesus criticised the Pharisees for following the law but having evil hearts/ Jesus said, 'The teachers of the law and the Pharisees sit in Moses' seat. So you must be careful

to do everything they tell you. But do not do what they do, for they do not practice what they preach.' (Matthew 23:2–3 [NIV]).

• Most Christians believe both good works and grace (through faith in Jesus) are needed to be saved/ you can't prove you have faith unless you show it in your outward behaviour/ a danger in believing in salvation through grace alone is that people can feel specially chosen so look down on others/ not feel they have to obey God's law as they are already 'saved'.

2 Practices

Test the 1 mark question

1. D) Liturgical worship

2. C) Christmas

Test the 2 mark question

Suggested answers, other relevant answers would be credited. 1 mark for each correct point.

3. By setting up charities/ Christian Aid/ CAFOD/ Tearfund/ by raising or donating money/ by working overseas in poor countries/ by praying for justice for the poor/ by campaigning for the poor.

4. Prayer helps Christians communicate with God/ develop and sustain their relationship with God/ thank God for blessings/ praise God/ ask God for help for oneself or others/ find courage to accept God's will in difficult times.

Test the 4 mark question

Suggested answers, other relevant answers would be credited. 1 mark for each simple contrasting or similar point, another mark for developing each point, so a maximum of 4 marks for two developed points.

6. *Ways must be contrasting*:

Infant baptism: Catholic, Orthodox, Anglican, Methodist and United Reformed Churches baptise babies/ 'I baptise you in the name of the Father, and of the Son, and of the Holy Spirit'/ blessed water poured over the baby's head/ sign of cross on baby's forehead/ anointing with oil/ white garment/ candle/ godparents' and parents' promises.

Believers' baptism: others such as Baptist and Pentecostal Christians baptise those who are old enough to make their own decision about baptism/ baptise people who have made a commitment to faith in Jesus/ full immersion in pool/ minister talks about meaning of baptism/ candidates are asked if they are willing to change their lives/ Bible passage/ brief testimony from candidate/ baptised 'in the name of the Father, and of the Son, and of the Holy Spirit'.

7. *Interpretations must be contrasting*:

Catholic, Orthodox and some Anglican Christians believe the bread and wine become the body and blood of Christ/ Jesus is fully present in the bread and wine/ a divine mystery/ those receiving become present in a mystical way at the death and resurrection of Christ/ receive God's grace/ Holy Communion is a sacrament.

Protestant Christians see Holy Communion as a reminder of Jesus' words and actions at the Last Supper/ bread and wine are symbols of Jesus' sacrifice/ they help them reflect on the meaning of Jesus' death and resurrection for their lives today/ it is an act of fellowship.

Test the 5 mark question

Suggested answers, other relevant answers would be credited. 1 mark for each simple contrasting or similar belief, another mark for developing each belief, so 4 marks for two developed beliefs, 1 extra mark for a correct reference to a source of religious belief or teaching.

9. Spreading the Christian gospel/ by public preaching/ by personal witness.

Evangelism is considered a duty of Christians because of the Great Commission/ 'Therefore go and make disciples of all nations, baptising them in the name of the Father and of the Son and of the Holy Spirit, and teaching them to obey everything I have commanded you' (Matthew 28:19–20 [NIV])/ people have a desire to share the good news with others because they have experienced it themselves.

Christians believe they are called to do more than just know Jesus in their own lives/ they are called to spread the good news to non-believers that Jesus is the Saviour of the world.

When the early disciples received the Spirit at Pentecost they were given the gifts necessary to carry out the Great Commission/ the Spirit gives some people wisdom/ knowledge/ faith/ gifts of healing/ miraculous powers/ prophecy/ the ability to speak in tongues and understand the message of those who speak in tongues.

10. Christians may work for reconciliation in their own lives by forgiving their enemies/ making up with people they have offended/ going to the sacrament of Reconciliation to be reconciled with God/ 'But I tell you, love your enemies and pray for those who persecute you' (Matthew 5:44 [NIV]).

Christians may work for reconciliation between political or religious groups through organisations/ e.g. through the Irish Churches Peace Project/ the Corrymeela Community/ which sought to bring Catholic and Protestant communities together in Northern Ireland/ through discussion and working on their differences together.

Christians could work for more global reconciliation through an organisation such as the Community of the Cross of Nails at Coventry Cathedral/ which works with partners in many countries/ to bring about peace and harmony in areas where conflict and violence are present.

Christians do this work because of Jesus' teaching and example/ as Paul says, 'For if, while we were God's enemies, we were reconciled to him through the death of his Son, how much more, having been reconciled, shall we be saved through his life!' (Romans 5:10 [NIV]).

Test the 12 mark question

Suggested answers shown here, but see page 10 for guidance on levels of response.

12. Arguments in support

• Going to a holy place/ a place where Jesus or saints lived and died can inspire people/ it can teach people more about their religion's history/ can strengthen faith as it increases knowledge about holy people/ Christians make pilgrimages to the Holy Land as it is where Jesus lived, preached, died and resurrected from the dead/ Christians can experience for themselves what it was like to live there/ they follow in the footsteps of Jesus/ meet others who share their faith/ the effort and discipline needed strengthens their faith.

• Some Christians go on pilgrimage to places where miracles are said to have occurred/ e.g. Lourdes in France/ they pray to be healed from sin/ mental or physical illness/ to thank God for a special blessing/ to help others who are disabled or ill, putting into practice love of neighbour.

• Some Christians go on pilgrimage to a remote place/ e.g. Iona in Scotland/ they go to have quiet time to pray/ read scriptures/ connect with God through nature/ reflect on their lives/ particularly if facing a big decision/ refresh their spiritual lives in today's busy world.

Arguments in support of other views

• Pilgrimage does not always bring people closer to God/ some places are very commercialised/ it can disappoint people who had a certain mental image of a place to see that it is touristy/ it can be very crowded so not a place for reflection/ some people on the pilgrimage may just see it as a holiday, making it hard to concentrate on God.

• Pilgrimage can be expensive/ not everyone can afford going abroad/ not everyone has time to make a pilgrimage, e.g. getting time off work/ family commitments.

• Other ways of becoming closer to God are better than pilgrimage/ daily prayer in one's own home can bring the peace of mind and heart the person needs/ receiving Holy Communion brings people closer to God than any journey/ going to the sacrament of Reconciliation can be done locally.

13. Arguments in support

• The Church (meaning all Christians) has a mission to spread the good news/ that Jesus Christ is the Son of God/ came into the world to be its saviour/ the Great Commission/ 'Therefore go and make disciples of all nations, baptising them in the name of the Father and of the Son and of the Holy Spirit, and teaching them to obey everything I have commanded you' (Matthew 28:19–20 [NIV]).

• Christians believe they are called to do more than just know Jesus in their own lives/ they are called to spread the good news to non-believers that Jesus is the Saviour of the world.

• When the early disciples received the Spirit at Pentecost they were given the gifts necessary to carry out the Great Commission/ the Spirit gives some people wisdom/ knowledge/ faith/ gifts of healing/ miraculous powers/ prophecy/ the ability to speak in tongues and understand the message of those who speak in tongues/ Christians today receive the Holy Spirit at their Confirmation/ they are called to be disciples of Jesus, like the first disciples/ so they must spread the faith fearlessly as the disciples did.

Arguments in support of other views

• The main job of a Christian is to believe in Jesus/ follow the commandments/ worship God/ love one's neighbour as oneself/ live a good life in the hope of eternal life in heaven.

• Many Christians do not have the personality to preach to others about their faith/ do not have the time if working/ have family responsibilities/ are not public speakers/ do not want to antagonise people who are unsympathetic non-believers/ cannot go abroad to work as missionaries.

• There are other ways of showing one's faith to others without actually 'telling them'/ being a good neighbour/ helping those in need/ working with charities/ worshipping God/ showing integrity/ having high moral principles that make non-believers notice that faith makes a difference to the Christian believer.

3 Relationships and families

Test the 1 mark question

1. D) Stability

2. B) A couple and their children

Test the 2 mark question

Suggested answers, other relevant answers would be credited. 1 mark for each correct point.

3. Men and women should be given the same rights/ all people are created equal by God/ 'love your neighbour' applies to everyone/ Christians follow Jesus' example in treating women with equal value/ 'There is neither Jew nor Gentile, neither slave nor free, nor is there male and female, for you are all one in Christ Jesus' (Galatians 3:28 [NIV])/ men and women can have different roles in the family but this does not mean they are not equal in God's sight/ Christian marriage is an equal partnership.

4. Most religions are against cohabitation (a couple living together and having a sexual relationship without being married)/ some Christians who oppose sex before marriage think cohabitation is sinful/ others believe it is a precious and important part of a marriage and should only be part of a life-long commitment/ Catholic and Orthodox

Churches believe a sexual relationship should only take place within marriage/ many Anglican and Protestant Christians accept that although marriage is best, people may live together in a faithful, loving, committed way without being married.

Test the 4 mark question

Suggested answers, other relevant answers would be credited. 1 mark for each simple contrasting or similar point, another mark for developing each point, so a maximum of 4 marks for two developed points.

6. *Beliefs must be contrasting:*

Christians believe marriage is for life/ vows made in the presence of God should not be broken/ Jesus taught that anyone who divorced and remarried was committing adultery (Mark 10:11–12)/ except in the case of adultery (Matthew 5:32)/ for Catholics marriage is a sacrament that is permanent/ cannot be dissolved by civil divorce/ Catholics can separate but cannot marry someone else while their partner is still alive.

Anglicans can marry someone else in church with the bishop's permission/ recognise that sometimes marriages fail/ divorce and remarriage is acceptable if those remarrying take the vows seriously/ this is the more compassionate thing to do/ Protestant Churches such as the Methodist and United Reformed Churches allow civil divorce and remarriage in church as long as the couple take the vows seriously/ they believe the Church should reflect the forgiveness of God/ accept people may have made a mistake and allow them a fresh start/ the Eastern Orthodox Church grants divorces and remarries couples, but usually not more than twice.

7. *Beliefs must be contrasting:*

Many Christians believe heterosexual relationships are part of God's plan for humans/ God created male and female/ told them to 'be fruitful and increase in number' (Genesis 1:28 [NIV])/ sex expresses a deep, life-long union best expressed in marriage/ some Christians oppose homosexual relationships because they go against God's plan/ go against the natural law because the relationship cannot produce children/ the Bible says it is wrong for a man to sleep with a man (Leviticus 18:22, 1 Corinthians 6:9–10)/ the Catholic Church teaches that homosexual sex is a sinful activity.

Some Christians think loving, faithful homosexual relationships are just as holy as heterosexual ones/ the Church of England welcomes homosexuals living in committed relationships/ God created all people and loves them equally.

Test the 5 mark question

Suggested answers, other relevant answers would be credited. 1 mark for each simple contrasting or similar belief, another mark for developing each belief, so 4 marks for two developed beliefs, 1 extra mark for a correct reference to a source of religious belief or teaching.

9. For Christians, procreation is an important purpose/ part of God's plan for humanity/ God created man and woman, blessed them and said, 'Be fruitful and increase in number; fill the earth and subdue it' (Genesis 1:28 [NIV])/ the family is where the basic needs of children are provided/ 'Children are a heritage from the Lord' (Psalms 127:3 [NIV]).

Protection is important/ keeping children safe from harm/ nurturing and caring for them/ stability is important/ the family is the building block of society/ where children learn how to be good citizens/ families keep society stable.

Educating children in a faith is important/ the family is where faith traditions are passed down to the next generation/ where children learn to love/ learn moral values/ caring for children's spiritual needs is important.

10. The Christian Church teaches that both parents and children have responsibilities in a family/ the commandment to 'Honour one's father and mother' (Exodus 20:12 [NIV]) applies to children of all ages/ it includes the respect and care given to the elderly members of the family/ 'Listen to your father who gave you life, and do not despise your mother when she is old' (Proverbs 23:22 [NIV])/ children should love, respect and obey their parents/ 'Children, obey your parents in everything, for this pleases the Lord' (Colossians 3:20 [NIV])/ parents have experience of life from which children can learn.

Test the 12 mark question

Suggested answers shown here, but see page 10 for guidance on levels of response.

12. Arguments in support

• Most Christians think marriage is the proper place to enjoy a sexual relationship/ sex expresses a deep, loving, lifelong union that first requires the commitment of marriage/ it is one of God's gifts at creation/ 'That is why a man leaves his father and mother and is united to his wife, and they become one flesh' (Genesis 2:24 [NIV]).

• Having sex is part of the trust between partners in marriage/ sex should not be a casual, temporary pleasure/ 'The sexual act must take place exclusively within marriage. Outside of marriage it always constitutes a grave sin' (Catechism 2390).

• Paul urged sexual restraint: 'Flee from sexual immorality. All other sins a person commits are outside the body, but whoever sins sexually, sins against their own body. Do you not know that your bodies are temples of the Holy Spirit, who is in you, whom you have received from God? You are not your own' (1 Corinthians 6:18–19 [NIV]).

• Marriage brings security in the faithfulness of the couple/ protects each partner's rights/ children benefit from the close relationship of the couple/ provides a stable environment in which to raise a family.

Arguments in support of other views

• Society has changed/ many people do not see sex as requiring the commitment of marriage/ contraception has reduced the risk of pregnancy before marriage/ many people engage in casual sexual relationships.

• The cost of marriage prevents some people from marrying immediately/ some couples want to see if the relationship is going to work before marrying/ some people do not think a marriage certificate makes any difference to their relationship.

- Some Christians accept that for some people sex before marriage is a valid expression of their love for each other/ some Christians may accept cohabitation, particularly if the couple is committed to each other/ more liberal Christians may accept that people may live together in a faithful, loving and committed way without being married.

- Atheists, humanists and non-religious people do not see marriage as a sacrament/ holy sign of God's love/ do not think marriage is necessary for a sexual relationship.

13. Arguments in support

- The Orthodox and Catholic Churches teach that using artificial contraception within marriage is wrong/ against natural law/ against the purpose of marriage to have children/ having children is God's greatest gift to a married couple/ 'Every sexual act should have the possibility of creating new life' (Humanae Vitae, 1968).

- God will not send more children than a couple can care for/ if Catholic couples wish to plan their families they should use a natural method, such as the rhythm method.

Arguments in support of other views

- Other Christians accept the use of artificial contraception provided it is not used to prevent having children altogether/ by mutual consent of the couple.

- It can be used for family planning/ for financial reasons (to prevent a child being born into deprivation)/ to protect the mother's health/ to protect the welfare of other children.

- Its use may allow a couple to develop their relationship before having children/ prevent sexually transmitted infections/ help reduce the population explosion.

- The Church of England approved the use of artificial contraception at the Lambeth Conference in 1930/ 'The Conference agrees that other methods may be used, provided that this is done in the light of Christian principles.'

4 Religion and life

Test the 1 mark question

1. C) A good or gentle death
2. B) Humans

Test the 2 mark question

Suggested answers, other relevant answers would be credited. 1 mark for each correct point.

3. Can only happen during the first 24 weeks of pregnancy unless the mother's life is in danger/ risk to mother's physical and mental health/ risk the baby is born with severe disabilities/ an additional child may endanger the physical or mental health of other children in the family/ must take place in an authorised clinic/ two doctors must agree.

4. A wonderful place where God resides/ a spiritual place with God/ eternal/ opposite from hell/ a place after death for the faithful/ includes all who repent/ a gift, not earned/ a state of happiness, no suffering, eternal peace.

Test the 4 mark question

Suggested answers, other relevant answers would be credited. 1 mark for each simple contrasting or similar point, another mark for developing each point, so a maximum of 4 marks for two developed points.

6. *Beliefs must be similar:*

Most Christians believe animal experimentation can be justified to help save human lives/ as it helps to make products safe for human use/ Christians believe humans have dominion/are more important than animals, so they can use animals for this purpose/ it is good stewardship of the earth's resources to use animals in this way/ as long as the animals suffer as little as necessary/ 'The righteous care for the needs of their animals' (Proverbs 12:10 [NIV]).

7. *Beliefs must be contrasting:*

Most Christians believe the earth's resources should be used responsibly so they exist for future generations/ this is good stewardship/ treating God's earth in the way he wants it to be treated/ 'The Lord God took the man (Adam) and put him in the Garden of Eden to work it and take care of it' (Genesis 2:15 [NIV])/ Adam's responsibility has been passed down to humankind.

Christians believe humans have been given dominion over the earth/ are the most important species on earth/ 'Rule over […] every living creature that moves on the ground' (Genesis 1:28 [NIV])/ some Christians believe this means they can use the earth's resources as they wish/ future generations will need to find alternatives.

Test the 5 mark question

Suggested answers, other relevant answers would be credited. 1 mark for each simple contrasting or similar belief, another mark for developing each belief, so 4 marks for two developed beliefs, 1 extra mark for a correct reference to a source of religious belief or teaching.

9. Christians believe it is a duty because God created the earth for humans to use and look after/ 'In the beginning God created the heavens and earth' (Genesis 1:1 [NIV])/ stewardship means humans have a responsibility to look after the earth on behalf of God/ God put Adam into the Garden of Eden 'to work it and take care of it' (Genesis 2:15 [NIV])/ it is an act of love to protect the earth for future generations/ the earth has great value and beauty, and humans are the only ones who can look after it.

10. Christians believe the universe was designed and made by God out of nothing/ the Bible states that God made the universe and all life in it in six days/ different things were created on different days, with humans last on day six/ 'In the beginning God created the heavens and earth' (Genesis 1:1 [NIV])/ *accept any other relevant quote*

from the Genesis 1 creation story/ most Christians believe the 'days' referred to in the creation story refer to longer periods of time/ God started the process of creation as the first cause, and used evolution to develop life to how it is now/ the Big Bang was used by God to create the universe so it wasn't chance or accident/ *creation stories from other religions are acceptable here.*

Test the 12 mark question

Suggested answers shown here, but see page 10 for guidance on levels of response.

12. Arguments in support

- The mother has to carry the baby, give birth to it and bring it up, so she should have the right to choose whether to continue with the pregnancy/ abortion should be a matter of personal choice/ making abortion easier gives more rights to the mother/ the mother's life is more important.

- Life doesn't start until birth (or from the point when the foetus can survive outside the womb), so abortion does not involve killing.

- It is cruel to allow a severely disabled child to be born/ to allow a child to be born into poverty/ if the child would have a very poor quality of life then abortion should be allowed/ some Christians would agree with this view.

- Allowing more abortions might help to reduce population growth/ reduce overcrowding/ prevent the earth's resources from being used up so fast.

Arguments in support of other views

- The current law is the best compromise between sides who support abortion and those that don't/ there is a reasonable balance between the rights of the mother and the unborn child/ so the law should not be changed.

- Many Christians believe abortion doesn't respect the sanctity of life/ Christians who believe life begins at the moment of conception think abortion is wrong, as it is taking away life given by God/ the law should be changed to make abortion harder.

- Disabled children can enjoy a good quality of life/ unwanted children can be adopted into families that will care for them/ those who choose abortion can suffer from depression and guilt afterwards.

13. Arguments in support

- A minority of Christians believe humans were given dominion over the earth so can do what they want with it/ 'Rule over the fish in the sea and the birds in the sky and over every living creature that moves on the ground' (Genesis 1:28 [NIV]).

- If resources are destroyed or used up, scientists will develop alternatives.

- Humans need natural resources to sustain their way of life.

Arguments in support of other views

- Most Christians believe humans were put on the earth as stewards to look after it on behalf of God for future generations/ God put Adam into the Garden of Eden 'to work it and take care of it' (Genesis 2:15 [NIV])/ it is wrong to destroy something that belongs to someone else (i.e. God).

- Many of the earth's natural resources are non-renewable so there is only a limited supply of them/ using them up too quickly will probably make life much harder for future generations/ this shows a lack of love and respect for others.

5 The existence of God and revelation

Test the 1 mark question

1. C) Theist
2. B) Mortal

Test the 2 mark question

Suggested answers, other relevant answers would be credited. 1 mark for each correct point.

3. The argument contradicts itself/ it says everything has a cause, but what caused God to exist?/ if God is eternal, why can't the universe be eternal?/ the Big Bang was a random event, not caused/ just because events on earth have causes does not necessarily mean the universe itself has a cause.

4. Disobedience of Adam and Eve/ misuse of freewill (e.g. war)/ natural causes (e.g. earthquakes, floods).

Test the 4 mark question

Suggested answers, other relevant answers would be credited. 1 mark for each simple contrasting or similar point, another mark for developing each point, so a maximum of 4 marks for two developed points.

6. *Beliefs must be contrasting:*

Christians believe miracles are events performed by God which appear to break the laws of nature/ *an example of such an event/* they confirm God's existence/ they show God is at work in the world.

They are not real/ they are lucky coincidences that have nothing to do with God/ may be made up for fame or money / healing miracles may be mind over matter or misdiagnosis/ can be explained scientifically in a way we don't yet know.

7. *Beliefs must be similar:*

Comes through ordinary human experiences/ through reason, conscience or morality/ through seeing God's creative work and presence in nature/ Christians believe God is revealed through his creation to be creative, all-knowing and powerful/ through worship or scripture/ the Bible can help to reveal what God is like and how he wants people to live/

the Bible reveals God to be powerful, just, loving and forgiving.

People are mistaken in interpreting normal events as general revelation/ nature is special but has nothing to do with revelation/ scriptures are opinions of their writers and not inspired by God/ scripture can be wrongly interpreted.

Test the 5 mark question

Suggested answers, other relevant answers would be credited. 1 mark for each simple contrasting or similar belief, another mark for developing each belief, so 4 marks for two developed beliefs, 1 extra mark for a correct reference to a source of religious belief or teaching.

9.	For Christians, a way of God directly revealing something about himself/ direct experience of God in an event, such as a vision or prophecy/ e.g. Moses receiving the Ten Commandments/ Mary finding out she is pregnant from the angel Gabriel/ Saul's vision/ can have a great influence on people's lives.

10.	Omnipotent/ omniscient/ benevolent/ immanent/ transcendent/ personal/ impersonal/ creator/ *any ideas in scripture related to creation, possibility of relationship with God through prayer, incarnation of Jesus, work of Holy Spirit.*

Test the 12 mark question

Suggested answers shown here, but see page 10 for guidance on levels of response.

**12.	Arguments in support**

•	Christians believe miracles are events with no natural or scientific explanation that only God could perform/ only God is all-powerful and transcendent, so only God is able to perform miracles.

•	If they occur as a response to prayer, they are a response to asking God for something/ prove that God is listening and responding to prayers.

•	They are usually good and God is the source of all that is good.

•	The fact that some people convert to Christianity after experiencing a miracle is proof of God's existence.

•	69 healing miracles have officially been recognised as taking place at Lourdes, proof of his power.

•	Miracles exist and are caused by God, therefore God exists.

Arguments in support of other views

•	Miracles are lucky coincidences and nothing to do with God.

•	Whether something counts as a miracle is a matter of interpretation.

•	They may have scientific explanations we haven't yet discovered.

•	Healings could be mind over matter or misdiagnosis.

•	Some miracles are made up for fame or money.

•	If God is involved in miracles, this means he is selective and unfair (as only a few people experience them)/ but God cannot be selective and unfair/ therefore he cannot be involved in miracles.

•	If miracles don't exist or have other explanations, they are nothing to do with God, so do not prove he exists.

**13.	Arguments in support**

•	A loving God would not allow people to suffer.

•	God should be aware of evil and suffering because he is omniscient/ if so, he should use his powers to prevent it because he is omnipotent/ because God does not do this, he cannot exist.

•	If God made all of creation to be perfect then there would not be earthquakes, droughts, etc./ suffering caused by the natural world is an example of poor design, which no good God would be responsible for.

Arguments in support of other views

•	It is unfair to blame God for suffering because he doesn't cause it.

•	Suffering is a result of the disobedience of Adam and Eve/ the result of humans misusing their free will.

•	If there was no evil, no one would be able to actively choose good over bad/ learn from their mistakes/ show compassion and kindness towards others who are suffering.

•	Humans are in charge of looking after the earth and God chooses not to interfere.

•	The existence of evil doesn't necessarily prove God does not exist, but could suggest he is not all-loving or all-powerful.

6 Religion, peace and conflict

Test the 1 mark question

1.	C) Justice

2.	D) Conventional weapons

Test the 2 mark question

Suggested answers, other relevant answers would be credited. 1 mark for each correct point.

3.	Just cause/ correct authority/ good intention/ last resort/ reasonable chance of success/ proportional methods used.

4.	For Christians violent protest goes against Jesus' teachings not to use violence/ goes against the commandment 'Do not kill'/ does not show 'love of neighbour'/ goes against the sanctity of life/ goes against 'So in everything, do to others what you would have them do to you, for this sums up the Law and the Prophets' (Matthew 7:12 [NIV]).

Test the 4 mark question

Suggested answers, other relevant answers would be credited. 1 mark for each simple contrasting or similar point, another mark for developing each point, so a maximum of 4 marks for two developed points.

6.	*Beliefs must be contrasting:*

Christians who support pacifism (e.g. The Religious Society of Friends – Quakers) believe that war can never be justified/ all killing is wrong/ it breaks the commandment 'You shall not murder' (Exodus 20:13 [NIV])/ Jesus taught 'Blessed are the peacemakers, for they shall be called children of God' (Matthew 5:9 [NIV])/ conflicts should be settled peacefully.

Christians who do not support pacifism believe that war is sometimes necessary as a last resort/ they would fight in a 'just war'/ to stop genocide taking place/ to defend one's country or way of life/ to help a weaker country defend itself from attack.

7.	*Beliefs must be similar:*

Forgiveness is showing grace and mercy/ pardoning someone for what they have done wrong/ Christians believe forgiveness is important as in the Lord's Prayer it says 'Forgive us our sins as we forgive those who sin against us'/ this means God will not forgive if Christians do not forgive others/ Christians believe God sets the example by offering forgiveness to all who ask for it in faith/ Christians believe there is no limit to the number of times they should forgive someone (Matthew 18:21–22).

Test the 5 mark question

Suggested answers, other relevant answers would be credited. 1 mark for each simple contrasting or similar belief, another mark for developing each belief, so 4 marks for two developed beliefs, 1 extra mark for a correct reference to a source of religious belief or teaching.

9.	Some Christians believe in the just war theory/ it is right to fight in a war if the cause is just/ war can be the lesser of two evils/ it can be justified if its purpose is to stop atrocities/ people have a right to self-defence/ 'If there is a serious injury, you are to take life for life, eye for eye, tooth for tooth' (Exodus 21:23–24 [NIV])/ 'Love your neighbour as yourself' (Matthew 22:39 [NIV]) demands protection of weaker allies through war.

10.	Reconciliation is a sacrament in the Catholic Church/ Christians believe it is important to ask God for forgiveness for sins/ reconciliation restores a Christian's relationship with God and other people.

Reconciliation is when individuals or groups restore friendly relations after conflict or disagreement/ it is important to build good relationships after a war so conflict does not break out again/ justice and peace must be restored to prevent further conflict/ to create a world which reflects God's intention in creation.

Christians believe they must be reconciled to others before they can worship God properly/ 'Therefore, if you are offering your gift at the altar and there remember that your brother or sister has something against you, leave your gift there in front of the altar. First go and be reconciled to them; then come and offer your gift' (Matthew 5:23–24 [NIV]).

Test the 12 mark question

Suggested answers shown here, but see page 10 for guidance on levels of response.

**12.	Arguments in support**

•	Some religious people believe in the concept of a holy war/ a holy war is fighting for a religious cause or God/ probably controlled by a religious leader/ these believers think that it is justifiable to defend their faith from attack.

•	Religion has been a cause of such wars in the past/ e.g. the Crusades, wars between Christians and Muslims, were fought over rights to the Holy Land/ in the Old Testament there are many references to God helping the Jews settle in the Promised Land at the expense of those already living there.

•	There are many examples of conflicts that involve different religious groups/ e.g. Catholics and Protestants in Northern Ireland during the 'Troubles'/ Israeli–Palestinian conflict/ conflict in India and Pakistan between Muslims and Hindus.

•	Some atheists claim that without religion, many conflicts could be avoided/ religiously motivated terrorism would cease.

Arguments in support of other views

•	Religion is not the main cause of wars: greed, self-defence and retaliation are all more common causes/ academic studies have found that religion plays a minor role in the majority of conflicts/ most wars have many causes/ e.g. opposition to a government/ economic reasons/ objection to ideological, political or social systems/ e.g. political differences played a greater role in the conflict in Northern Ireland than religion.

•	Christians today believe they should defend their faith by reasoned argument, not violence/ many Christians think no war can be considered 'holy' when there is great loss of life/ "Put your sword back in its place," Jesus said, 'for all who draw the sword die by the sword" (Matthew 26:52 [NIV])/ 'You have heard that it was said to the people long ago, 'You shall not murder […] But I tell you that anyone who is angry with a brother or sister will be subject to judgement' (Matthew 5:21–22 [NIV]).

**13.	Arguments in support**

•	Religious people should be the main peacemakers because of their beliefs/ e.g. Christians believe in 'love your neighbour'/ the sanctity of life/ equality/ justice/ peace/ forgiveness/ reconciliation/ Jesus taught 'Blessed are the peacemakers' (Matthew 5:9 [NIV]).

•	Prayer and meditation can bring inner peace to individuals/ this helps avoid quarrels with others/ peacemaking begins with each person.

•	Many religious people are engaged in peacemaking in today's world/ e.g. the Anglican Pacifist Fellowship works to raise awareness of the issue of pacifism/ the 'Peace People' (Mairead Corrigan, Betty Williams and Ciaran McKeown) in Northern Ireland work to bring the Catholic and Protestant communities together to stop violence.

Arguments in support of other views

• Religious people should be peacemakers, but not the main ones/ the problems of global conflict require global solutions that are beyond any individual to solve/ the United Nations should be the main peacekeeping organisation/ only large organisations or governments with powerful resources can hope to affect peacemaking in the world.

• Religious people can be peacemakers in their own families and support justice and peace groups locally, but they cannot take the lead as peacemakers/ their main duty is to their family/ people have jobs that do not allow them to stop violence across the world/ the most they can do is contribute to organisations which help.

• Everyone should take equal responsibility for helping to contribute towards peace, whether they are religious or not/ some situations might benefit from peacemakers who are not religious.

7 Religion, crime and punishment

Test the 1 mark question

1. A) Corporal punishment

2. C) Happiness

Test the 2 mark question

Suggested answers, other relevant answers would be credited. 1 mark for each correct point.

3. Retribution/ deterrence/ reformation/ protection.

4. Poverty/ upbringing/ mental illness/ addiction/ greed/ hate/ opposition to an unjust law.

Test the 4 mark question

Suggested answers, other relevant answers would be credited. 1 mark for each simple contrasting or similar point, another mark for developing each point, so a maximum of 4 marks for two developed points.

6. *Beliefs must be contrasting:*

Approved of by most Christians and many religious people/ as allows offenders to make up for what they have done wrong/ helps to reform and rehabilitate offenders/ may involve counselling, treatment or education/ may include an opportunity to apologise to the victim/ no harm is done to the offender.

Some religious people disapprove of community service as it is not a sufficient deterrent/ there is no element of retribution/ it is too soft a punishment.

7. *Beliefs must be similar:*

It makes reoffending unlikely/ brings justice as the punishment matches the fate of the victim/ deters others from committing serious crimes/ 'life for life, eye for eye, tooth for tooth' (Exodus 21:23–24 [NIV])/ Muslims have similar beliefs (Qur'an 5:45).

Test the 5 mark question

Suggested answers, other relevant answers would be credited. 1 mark for each simple contrasting or similar belief, another mark for developing each belief, so 4 marks for two developed beliefs, 1 extra mark for a correct reference to a source of religious belief or teaching.

9. Christians are expected to forgive those who offend against them and if they do God will forgive them/ forgiveness is not a replacement for punishment/ it should be unlimited/ 'not seven times, but seventy-seven times' (Matthew 18:22 [NIV])/ Jesus forgave those who crucified him and Christians should follow his example/ 'Father forgive them, for they do not know what they are doing' (Luke 23:34 [NIV])/ forgiveness is emphasised in the Lord's Prayer ('forgive us our sins as we forgive those who sin against us').

10. Hate crimes are condemned by Christianity/ hate crimes target individuals and groups perceived to be different/ Christians believe God created all humans equal in his image/ 'There is neither Jew nor Gentile, slave nor free man, male nor female, for you are all one in Christ Jesus' (Galatians 3:28 [NIV])/ hate crimes are not loving/ 'Love your neighbour as yourself' (Mark 12:31 [NIV])/ hate crimes usually involve violence or killing/ 'You shall not murder' (Exodus 20:13 [NIV]).

Test the 12 mark question

Suggested answers shown here, but see page 10 for guidance on levels of response.

12. **Arguments in support**

• Sanctity of life means life is sacred and special to God/ should be valued and respected/ the life of an offender has equal value to any other life/ the use of the death penalty does not respect life.

• Sanctity of life also suggests that only God has the right to take life/ this means it is not right to take another person's life/ this interferes with God's plan for a person's life.

Arguments in support of other views

• Murderers have already taken the life of someone else so their life should not be respected.

• Executing a murderer ensures they don't go on to kill again, thus preserving the sanctity of life/ the death penalty may deter others from killing and breaking the sanctity of life.

• 'Whoever sheds human blood, by humans shall their blood be shed' (Genesis 9:6 [NIV]) overrides the sanctity of life/ as does 'life for life, eye for eye, tooth for tooth' (Exodus 21:23–24 [NIV]).

• For those who don't believe in God, sanctity of life does not show that the death penalty is wrong/ there are other reasons for why the death penalty is wrong/ e.g. it is

not an effective deterrent/ it does not allow for the possibility of reformation/ it may kill innocent people.

13. **Arguments in support**

• Committing crime is wrong whatever the reason/ all crime causes someone to suffer.

• People should obey the law/ God put the system of government in place to rule every citizen so it is his law that is being broken (Romans 13:31).

• Christians believe it is wrong to commit crime because of poverty/ people should focus on creating a fairer society where the need to steal because of poverty is removed.

• Those who commit crime through illness or addiction should be provided with treatment so they have no reason to commit crimes.

• People who want to protest against an unjust law can do so legally, e.g. through a peaceful protest.

Arguments in support of other views

• Society is not fair so crimes because of need or poverty are justified in some circumstances/ e.g. it may be better to steal food than allow a child to starve.

• Some laws are unjust and the only way to change them is to break them/ peaceful protest is not always powerful enough to change the law.

• All humans have a tendency to do bad things, including crime, because of original sin.

• Those who commit crime because of addiction/mental illness cannot help it.

8 Religion, human rights and social justice

Test the 1 mark question

1. C) Unfairly judging someone before the facts are known

2. B) Promoting tolerance

Test the 2 mark question

Suggested answers, other relevant answers would be credited. 1 mark for each correct point.

3. Unfair pay/ bad working conditions/ bad housing/ poor education/ high interest rates on loans or credit cards/ people trafficking/ modern slavery.

4. Give to the Church for its upkeep and mission/ help people in need/ donate to charities.

Test the 4 mark question

Suggested answers, other relevant answers would be credited. 1 mark for each simple contrasting or similar point, another mark for developing each point, so a maximum of 4 marks for two developed points.

6. *Beliefs must be contrasting:*

Christianity teaches that prejudice is always wrong because it is unjust to single out individuals or groups for inferior treatment/ some Christians believe any relationship based on love should be cherished.

Some Christians think homosexual relationships are unnatural and against the Bible/ Adam and Eve were male and female/ homosexual relationships cannot lead to the 'natural' creation of a child.

7. *Beliefs must be similar:*

The Bible stresses the importance of providing human rights to all people/ which includes creating a more just society/ 'Let justice roll on like a river' (Amos 5:24)/ Christians believe it is not loving to deny people their rights/ rights are written into law, and the law is inspired by God so must be obeyed/ Christians have a responsibility to help provide human rights/ 'faith without deeds is useless' (James 2:20 [NIV]).

Test the 5 mark question

Suggested answers, other relevant answers would be credited. 1 mark for each simple contrasting or similar belief, another mark for developing each belief, so 4 marks for two developed beliefs, 1 extra mark for a correct reference to a source of religious belief or teaching.

9. Poverty is sometimes caused by injustice and Christians must combat injustice/ poverty involves suffering and Christians are expected to help relieve suffering/ e.g. the Parable of the Sheep and the Goats/ people have God-given talents that they should use to help overcome poverty/ e.g. the Parable of the Talents/ e.g. the Parable of the Rich man and Lazarus/ tackling poverty is good stewardship/ Jesus' teaching to 'love your neighbour' encourages Christians to help those in poverty.

10. Christianity teaches that wealth can lead to traits such as greed and selfishness/ 'For the love of money is a root of all kinds of evil' (1 Timothy 6:10 [NIV])/ focusing on wealth brings the danger of ignoring God and neglecting the spiritual life/ 'You cannot serve both God and money' (Matthew 6:24 [NIV])/ this can make it harder to get into heaven/ 'It is easier for a camel to go through the eye of a needle than for someone who is rich to enter the kingdom of God' (Mark 10:25 [NIV])/ Jesus told a rich man to sell all he had and give it to the poor in order to have treasure in heaven.

Test the 12 mark question

Suggested answers shown here, but see page 10 for guidance on levels of response.

12. **Arguments in support**

• Discrimination is an action that can cause physical and psychological harm/ goes against the ideas of equality/justice/human rights/ all of which are central to Christian ethics.

- Christianity teaches that all people should be treated equally because they are all made in God's image/ 'There is neither Jew nor Gentile, neither slave nor free, nor is there male and female, for you are all one in Christ Jesus' (Galatians 3:28 [NIV]).

- Positive discrimination is still a form of discrimination/ it would be better to treat all people equally.

Arguments in support of other views

- Positive discrimination helps to make up for centuries of negative discrimination against minority groups/ helps to make people aware of the need to rectify negative discrimination against minority groups.

- Positive discrimination helps those with disabilities to live more equally alongside people without disabilities/ shows love and compassion to people who are suffering/ so it can be supported by Christian teachings.

- It is important to differentiate between the needs of different people/ not everyone is the same/ some people are better suited to certain roles than others.

13. Arguments in support

- Freedom of religion is a basic human right/ 'Everyone has the right to freedom of thought, conscience and religion' (The United Declaration of Human Rights)/ in the UK the law allows people to follow whichever faith they choose.

- It is wrong to try to force someone to follow a religion/ or to prevent them from following a religion/ it should be a matter of personal choice/ this makes choosing to follow a particular religion more significant or meaningful.

- Forcing people to follow a religion or preventing them from following a religion could lead to more conflict and fighting between different religions.

- Being a Christian is a choice that any person can make/ Christians believe religious freedom is important/ Jesus taught people to show tolerance and harmony.

Arguments in support of other views

- If a religion teaches hatred and intolerance, there should be limits on how it can be taught or practised/ people should not be allowed to join it for the wrong reasons.

- Some people might argue that to show patriotism, a person should follow the main religion in their country.

- Some people might argue that when people are allowed to join any religion, this can lead to conflict and tension between different religious groups, whereas if everyone followed the same religion then there would be more harmony between people.

- Everybody also has the right not to follow any religion.